RELATIVE/OUTSIDER

Recent Titles in
Contemporary Studies in Social and Policy Issues in Education: The
David C. Anchin Center Series (formerly Social and Policy Issues in
Education: The David C. Anchin Center Series)
Kathryn M. Borman, Series Editor

Knowledge and Pedagogy: The Sociology of Basil Bernstein
Alan R. Sadovnik, editor

Assessment, Testing, and Evaluation in Teacher Education
Suzanne Wegener Soled, editor

Reinventing the University: A Radical Proposal for a Problem-Focused University
Jan Sinnott and Lynn Johnson

Schoolteachers and Schooling: Ethoses in Conflict
Eugene F. Provenzo, Jr., and Gary N. McCloskey

Implementing Educational Reform: Sociological Perspectives on Educational Policy
Kathryn M. Borman, Peter W. Cookson, Jr., Alan Sadovnik, and Jean Spade, editors

Maps, Metaphors, and Mirrors: Moral Education in Middle School
Carol K. Ingall

The Minority Voice in Educational Reform: An Analysis by Minority and Women
College of Education Deans
Louis A. Castenell and Jill M. Tarule, editors

Pathways to Privatization in Education
Joseph Murphy, Scott W. Gilmer, Richard Weise, and Ann Page

Comparative Higher Education: Knowledge, the University, and Development
Philip G. Altbach

Building Moral Communities Through Educational Drama
Betty Jane Wagner, editor

Development of the Social Sciences in the United States and Canada:
The Role of Philanthropy
Theresa Richardson and Donald Fisher, editors

Stories Out of School: Memories and Reflections on Care and Cruelty in the
Classroom
James L. Paul and Terry Jo Smith, editors

RELATIVE/OUTSIDER

The Art and Politics of Identity Among Mixed Heritage Students

Kendra R. Wallace

Contemporary Studies in Social and Policy Issues in Education:
The David C. Anchin Center Series
Kathryn M. Borman, Series Editor

ABLEX PUBLISHING
Westport, Connecticut · London

Library of Congress Cataloging-in-Publication Data

Wallace, Kendra R.
  Relative/outsider : the art and politics of identity among mixed heritage students /
Kendra R. Wallace.
     p.   cm. — (Contemporary studies in social and policy issues in education)
  Includes bibliographical references and index.
  ISBN 1–56750–550–3 (alk. paper) — ISBN 1–56750–551–1 (pbk. : alk. paper)
     1. Minorities—Education—United States—Case studies.   2. Racially mixed
people—Education—United States—Case studies.   3. Ethnic relations—United States—Case
studies.   I. Title.   II. Series.
  LC3731.W35   2001
  371.829′00973—dc21   00–049343

British Library Cataloguing in Publication Data is available.

Copyright © 2001 by Kendra R. Wallace

All rights reserved. No portion of this book may be
reproduced, by any process or technique, without the
express written consent of the publisher.

Library of Congress Catalog Card Number: 00–049343
ISBN:1–56750–550–3
        1–56750–551–1 (pbk.)

First published in 2001

Ablex Publishing, 88 Post Road West, Westport, CT 06881
An imprint of Greenwood Publishing Group, Inc.
www.ablexbooks.com

Printed in the United States of America

The paper used in this book complies with the
Permanent Paper Standard issued by the National
Information Standards Organization (Z39.48–1984).

10 9 8 7 6 5 4 3 2 1

This book is dedicated to my nieces
Kelsey, Cassidy, and Korinne Wallace
who are joyful reminders of the beauty in human diversity

Contents

Preface

This is an exploratory study of identity development among students of recently mixed heritage. The stories presented offer insights into the discourses that these students construct around ethnic and racial identity. Their accounts poignantly illustrate how the social categories of race and ethnicity remain important identity markers at the close of the twentieth century. Yet the experiences of these students reveal how these identity markers continue to undergo reconstitution and redefinition at this point in U.S. history.

This book details how a group of recently mixed heritage students come to understand ethnic and racial difference over the course of their lives. While the study considers the variation and commonalities among students' experiences, it does not attempt to advance a universal model of ethnoracial identity development for mixed heritage people. I hope the stories assembled provide a basis for better understanding the complexity of these students' lives, as well as the kaleidoscopic nature of ethnic and racial life in the United States. The book will be of interest to researchers and students in the social sciences, as well as individuals and groups concerned with questions of diversity, identity, and schooling in cross-cultural contexts.

I have no doubt that my own background as a first generation, mixed heritage woman clearly influences this research. I suspect that through the process of meeting and interviewing these individuals, I was able to establish a greater sense of rapport with students than would be possible for a researcher from a monoethnic/ racial background. Inevitably, participants asked questions about my identity and experiences. There were also times when I found myself on common ground with a student and I ventured to share aspects of my life in response to their comments. These moments deepened the value of the interviews in a way that could not have been achieved through a simple reading of the prepared interview probes. I believe the reciprocal nature of the interviews made this a richly rewarding, transformative experience for all involved.

Finally, finding the best words to discuss the dynamic identities of these students remains a challenge. I become uneasy using racial terminology even though it is fundamental to this work. My discomfort stems from the way race projects an illusion of order as it obscures those experiences and identities which fail to fit neatly within its parameters. By using racial terminology, I in no way mean to suggest the existence of discrete and homogeneous biological races of people. To the contrary, this work tries to describe the cacophony of ethnic and racial life in the United States, and the nonsynchronous ethnoracial experiences that are often muted when we resort to the essentializing language of race. So I find myself dancing with this tension throughout the work as I attempt to use the language of race to portray how our social worlds, the cognitive maps we construct, become inhabited by racialized interpretations.

The term *mixed heritage* is used in the book to refer to recent (first, second, and third generation) multiple ethnic and racial heritage. I would like to stress that I do not equate race with ethnicity. However, I will use racial terminology to connote the many social meanings it carries among the participants and the larger society, including references to ethnicity and ethnic identity, however imprecise this may be. When I refer to students' multiple heritages (such as Asian or black) I do so with the understanding that these are intrinsically diverse and unstable social categories. While race can be used to imply a pan-ethnic or diasporic identity, I find it important to use ethnic nomenclature since it is emphasized by the students themselves, especially among those who have more recent ties to indigenous communities and/or to communities outside of the United States.

Throughout the coming chapters, I have tried to incorporate the students' vocabulary, as well as my own, when describing their experiences. Students generally describe their ethnoracial heritage and identities through blended references. One may state, for example, that "I am both Venezuelan and Cambodian" or "I am Japanese and black," thereby referencing each heritage community. The word *mixed* is frequently used as well (e.g., "I'm mixed" to connote both Venezuelan and Cambodian or Japanese and black) to describe one's heritage and identity.

The following are some frequently used terms that will appear in this study:

Biracial/ethnic. Having recent ancestry from two ethnoracial groups; a word to describe the dual ethnic or racial nature of one's heritage and/or identity; here synonymous with multiethnic/racial.

Ethnic. Pertaining to the lifeways of a social group defined by a common ancestry, culture, geographic origins, and sometimes religion.

Ethnic identity. The dimension of a person's overall self-concept, or sense of self, that develops out of an understanding of their membership within a particular ethnic group, and the meaning that this membership conveys; ethnic identity does not simply mean one's ethnicity, or ethnic group of heritage.

Ethnoracial. Referring to both ethnic and racial elements.

First generation biracial/ethnic. Having birthparents who self-identify as monoracial/ethnic; same as immediately biracial/ethnic.

Immediately biracial/ethnic. Having birthparents who self-identify as monoracial/ethnic; same as first generation biracial/ethnic.

Interracial/ethnic. Involving elements across ethnoracial groups perceived to be distinct.

Mixed. A composite of elements from two or more ethnoracial communities perceived to be distinct.

Mixed heritage. Here refers to having recent, multiple ethnic and racial heritage.

Monoethnic/racial. Having ancestry or an identity orientation grounded in one ethnoracial group.

Multiethnic/racial. Having recent ancestry in multiple ethnoracial groups; a word to describe the multiple ethnic or racial nature of one's heritage and/or identity; here synonymous with biracial/ethnic.

Race. A sociopolitical category that changes over time and refers to perceived biological and social commonalities of a group of people; a system of classification that organizes people into groups according to characteristics perceived to be shared by the group (including phenotype, genotype, culture, and other criteria).

Recently mixed. While recognizing the fact that race is a specious concept, and that most people are "mixed" genetically, here this phrase refers to individuals of first, second, or third generation mixed ethnoracial heritage.

Whole heritage. A term used to connote having same heritage parents.

Acknowledgments

A couple of years ago, while browsing at a bookstore in Berkeley, I was surprised to find my name in a book written by a woman who had interviewed me two years prior. At the time of the interview, the author told me she was writing an article on the emergent mixed heritage, or multiracial movement. Standing in the bookstore, I recalled how during the interview it quickly became evident that she disapproved of lobbyists working to change the existing categories of race/ethnicity to recognize interracial/ethnic families and individuals. The bias underlying her questions was blatant, and I soon began to turn the questions back on my interviewer. She abruptly ended our conversation and after several fruitless inquiries I assumed that the article never materialized.

The book she was writing was *Bulletproof Diva: Tales of Race, Sex, and Hair* (1995) and the author was Lisa Jones, a first generation black–white woman who writes frequently on this topic from a perspective condemning mixed heritage activists as idealists and opportunists. Her critique exemplifies a common response by media and researchers alike to the articulation of mixed heritage identities. At the heart of this critique lies the assumption that people are physically and metaphysically bound to one community of heritage. In her book, the caricatures Jones crafts of individuals who identify with their mixed heritage are very familiar because they have long roots within our society's racial ecology. It is within this ecology that we learn to associate ourselves and others as organically rooted in distinct racial territories. Since people are presumed to be members of a single community, miscegenation symbolizes the rupture of group boundaries, and those who claim a mixed identity symbolize social and psychic displacement.

Like other minorities, the lives of mixed heritage individuals are subject to interpretation and distortion by others who rely upon well-worn stereotypes that are deeply woven into the fabric of our racial life. As in the Jones case described, attempts to engage in critical discussions about contemporary mixed heritage experiences are often hampered by conventional race wisdom. Over the course of my life I have met dozens of individuals who, like myself, grew up in the metaphorical borderlands between ethnic and racial communities. Our collective experiences reflect a range of identity approaches that I have yet to see adequately treated in any one volume. My experience with Jones served to reinforce my determination to research how post-1960s mixed heritage people in the United States come to view identity, belonging, and community on their own terms and in their own words.

I would like to express my most sincere appreciation to the fifteen students whose lives are the focus of this study. I will always be grateful for their trust in me and for raising their own voices in support of this work. I hope that the experience was as rewarding for them as it has been for me.

I want to thank my husband and family for their loving encouragement that has seen me through this process. Many thanks go to my colleagues at the University of Maryland, Baltimore County (UMBC). I would like to convey my appreciation for the advice shared by Susan Blunck, Jodi Crandall, Signithia Fordham, Bill Johnson, John Lee, and Wendy Saul on this project. And a special thank you goes to James Rutkowski in the UMBC Education Department for his technological assistance.

At Stanford University, I would like to acknowledge the powerful insights and incredible guidance extended to me by John Baugh, David Fetterman, Renato Rosaldo, and David Tyack. Finally, I thank Ron Glass at Arizona State University West, the founding members of the Multiracial Alternatives Project at the University of California–Berkeley, Byron Williams, and my many friends for their support during this project.

Chapter 1

Introduction

> A high school principal in Wedowee, Alabama, holds an assembly for eleventh and twelfth grade students to determine the potential for interracial dating at the upcoming prom. When a dozen or so students reply that they will be attending with a partner of a different race, Principal Hullond Humphries proposes to cancel the dance, citing recent interracial tensions on the campus. This prompts the president of the junior class, a young biracial black–white woman named ReVonda Bowen, to ask the principal, "Who am I supposed to take?" The principal allegedly responds by saying that his decision to call off the prom, rather than permit interracial couples to attend, is designed to prevent such a "mistake"—a mistake he implies was made by Bowen's parents.
>
> Based on Harrison 1994

Nearly thirty years after the last antimiscegenation laws were nullified by the U.S. Supreme Court, the story above speaks to this society's continued preoccupation with race and race mixing. The Bowen incident struck many people as appalling not just because the incident occurred in 1993, but also because the Wedowee school board did virtually nothing to rebuke this racial affront; the principal was merely given a two-week suspension with pay. Various civil rights groups rallied in support of Bowen, arguing that her rights were

violated when Humphries demeaned her heritage. Bowen subsequently filed a civil lawsuit against Humphries, whose high school
was destroyed by arson within the year following the incident.

That same year, the cover of *Time* magazine featured a computer-
generated image of an ethnoracially mixed woman, her lightly
tanned skin, fine sandy-brown hair, and petite features touted as
"The New Face of America" (*Time* Special Issue, Fall 1993). The
burgeoning media attention to interracial/ethnic topics in the 1990s
coincides with the visibility of celebrities, such as Tiger Woods, Dean
Cain, Mariah Carey, and Derek Jeter who openly discuss their recently mixed heritage. Such media coverage over the changing "face"
of race indicates a budding awareness about interracial/ethnic families and mixed heritage individuals, whose growing numbers are
beginning to blur the makeup of our racial categories in the United
States (Root 1992).

In a nation that is quite clearly multiethnic and multiracial, these
developments should not seem particularly extraordinary. But the
Time cover and the Bowen incident poignantly illustrate how, once
made visible, contemporary interracial/ethnic realities are prone
to interpretations that alternately vilify or glorify people who transgress the borders of race and ethnic group identity. Just where do
recently mixed heritage people fit into the schema of intergroup
relations in contemporary U.S. society? More important to this work,
where do they see themselves as fitting and why? Perhaps individuals of mixed descent simply view themselves as belonging in
one or the other group, or perhaps both. Maybe they see themselves
as "edge-walkers" occupying a third space, the place Gloria Anzaldúa
describes as the borderlands "betwixt and between" different communities where diverse elements come together and contribute to
syncretic identities (Anzaldúa 1987; Krebs 1999). This project is
concerned with how fifteen students of recently mixed ancestry
answer this question, and what their responses reveal about ethnic and racial life in the late twentieth-century United States.

RECENT INTERRACIAL/
INTERETHNIC TRENDS

The Biracial Baby Boom

Since 1970, the U.S. census has witnessed a doubling in the rate
of interracial/ethnic marriage, resulting in the 1990 census esti-
mate of 2.7 million marriages between interracially/ethnically identified, heterosexual partners (Saluter 1992). These unions have
pushed the rate of mixed heritage births to surpass that of single

race births by 245 percent since the early 1970s, a first in U.S. history (Saluter 1992; Root 1996). In 1990, the estimated number of biracial/ethnic children living in mixed households was reported to be 4 million. While still a relatively small proportion of all births, the boom in the number of children born to interracial partners presents a challenge to our society's current five-race framework, a challenge that is clearly noted·by the U.S. Bureau of the Census. Approximately 250,000 individuals added their own "multiracial designator" to describe their race on the 1990 census, while the "other" category grew at the fastest rate (45 percent), in part due to the growing numbers of recently mixed race individuals (Root 1996; Omi 1997). In response to recent efforts to alter census categories of race and ethnicity, the Office of Management and Budget (OMB) has agreed to change federal guidelines for collecting data on the 2000 census in recognition of the burgeoning number of first and second generation people of mixed heritage (Saluter 1992).

The "biracial baby boom" (Root 1992) is a unique development in the course of U.S. race relations with origins borne out of a changing social climate distinguished by a resurgence in racial pride and equal rights movements. The Civil Rights movement of the 1950s and 1960s carved out unprecedented opportunities for integration within workplaces, educational institutions, and communities in general, setting the stage for increased consensual interracial relationships. These opportunities, combined with the eradication of antimiscegenation laws in 1967 and steadily rising immigration rates during this era, contributed to a boom in the population of first generation, mixed heritage individuals raised within interracial/ethnic family structures and communities. The mixed heritage students in this study grew up at a time in U.S. history when an emergent multiculturalism was gaining currency in the mass media and K–12 curricula. While the merits of popular multiculturalism and its early melting pot ideology are contentious, its idealistic and egalitarian framework is nonetheless one of its most enduring features, as you will see in these students' stories.

A Challenge to the Racial Order

Interracial/ethnic families are becoming a growing presence in a society that does not readily accommodate them or their mixed heritage children beyond the traditional system of hypodescent, or the "one-drop" rule, which technically applies only to part white–European individuals. Alongside the increased media attention over the past decade there has been a groundswell of scholarship on interracial/ethnic topics taking the form of empirical studies, publications, higher-education courses, seminars, as well as projects and conferences sponsored by college groups around the country. And until recently, there was very little research available for educators interested in the developmental experiences of mixed heritage students.

From a theoretical standpoint, the surge in scholarship is in direct reaction to much of the earlier research conducted on mixed heritage children and adolescents, guided as it was by an unwavering dependence on one-drop logic and its mutually exclusive notions of ethnic and racial identity. Contemporary theories of ethnic and racial identity generated over the past three decades often presume development to be linear, static, and limited to a single reference group.[1] Even more recent popular models of biculturalism fall prey to this either–or logic and can render multiple or ambiguous ethnic self-identifications as deviant.

When brought to bear on recently mixed populations, such models encourage psychological analyses and interventions that tend to problematize a mixed heritage person's orientation by requiring their conformity to externally determined standards. Contemporary identity theories, therefore, tend to reinforce existing societal taboos around interracial sex and marriage as unnatural, and perpetuate negative stereotypes about mixed heritage children as marginal people. Similar to the criticism wrought by minority researchers against cultural deficit theories in the 1960s and 1970s, researchers (many of whom are of mixed heritage) are now challenging popular identity theories as inadequate and oppressive structures when applied to recently mixed populations.

The Mixed Heritage Movement

The 1990s has witnessed a successful organization of individuals from a wide range of mixed heritage backgrounds. Driven by a collective of interracial/ethnic family and student groups, the mixed heritage movement (sometimes called the multiracial movement) has organized to ensure the freedom of self-identification and accurate third-party representation in a manner consistent with the experiences and medical concerns of recently mixed people. The primary goal of the movement has been the discontinuation of mutually exclusive categories in U.S. census and other forms beginning in the year 2000. This relatively narrow political agenda flies in the face of conventional identity politics since the post–neo-Civil Rights era, which have been predicated upon the existence of recognizable and mutually exclusive social groups. Because such an agenda has the potential to destabilize the very categories upon which so many social policies and movements rest, the movement has been discredited by some minority communities suspicious of its motives and fearful of its demographic consequences (Jones 1995; Azoulay 1997). Meanwhile, the mainstream media has depicted the mixed heritage movement as a salve to our society's contentious race relations or a bane to researchers and demographers alike.

Despite its unconventional cause and unlikely composition, the movement has been able to gain credibility within the political arena by positioning recently mixed heritage people as an unlikely group whose members share the oppressive and marginalizing effects of mutually exclusive categories. In this way, the movement bears the earmarks of other contemporary identity projects as its members align themselves and assert their cause out of a common experience and sense of being different from others. Yet the difference in this case is at the individual level, as movement supporters recognize the possibility of diversity within the individual and frequent marginalization from all ethnic and racial centers (Zack 1995). The mixed heritage movement simultaneously rails against prevailing strategies of identity politics which require such an undesirable stasis, or what Stuart Hall calls the "necessary closure" a group needs within the public sphere if they are to achieve a specific political goal (Hall 1994). Therefore, the mixed heritage movement is a paradox in the contemporary climate of identity politics as it represents a collective of individuals who unify around their individual diversity and generally refuse to be reified as a group.

STORIES FROM ACROSS THE MARGINS

Much has been written about popular multiculturalism's shortcomings in the area of education (Giroux 1992; Glass and Wallace 1996). As McCarthy and Crichlow (1993) contend, attempts to critically address issues of power, identity, and the nature of knowledge in education have been rearticulated through a mainstream multiculturalist lens that oversimplifies the complexity of human diversity and largely ignores inequalities that are reproduced through schooling processes. The language of multiculturalism reifies the master concepts of diversity, such as race, gender, class, and so forth, despite their intrinsic volatility. Most educators, for example, address racial inequalities within schools by crafting a popular multiculturalism that locates the source of the problem at the level of individual racism, leaving untouched any consideration of the systemic nature of these disparities.

Roman (1993) contends that in order to challenge racism we must engage in scholarship that exposes race as an unstable concept in its day to day expression. This study takes up the challenge by exploring the diverse experiences of fifteen students from recently mixed heritage backgrounds. Their stories speak volumes about the unstable nature of race and ethnic identity in contemporary U.S. society.

Overview of the Study

In this book I talk with fifteen high school and university students from many different types of mixed heritage backgrounds. Based on an interview study, this work explores how these individuals come to make sense of their ethnoracial identities across the contexts of home, family, school, and community (used here to mean both local and diasporic). Often overlooked in research on race and mixed race, the book considers the nature and import of ethnic identity as it is nurtured through students' experiences at home and in the broader ethnic community. It also examines the interplay of racial identity formation and ethnic identity development. Finally, the book addresses the role of schooling contexts within these developmental trajectories and suggests several implications for educational policy and practice.

The recruitment process for this study was not a simple process. I was interested in attracting a range of mixed heritage students who may have vastly differing perceptions about their ethnoracial identities. Yet any attempt to select a mixed heritage sample will inevitably attract subjects who already self-identify as multiracial/ethnic (Root 1992). This study attempted to minimize this tendency by stressing biracial/ethnic *heritage* from biracial/ethnic *self-identification* on the initial race/ethnicity survey and subsequent recruitment flyer (Appendixes A and B).

Data were collected during an eight-month period spanning from April through December 1996. The race/ethnicity survey was developed as a vehicle for recruiting subjects of mixed heritage and is a comprehensive approach for collecting data on both racial and ethnic heritage.[2] It consists of five general racial categories which, at that time, corresponded with the Office of Management and Budget's framework, and each category featured multiple ethnic subcategories as well as open-ended spaces for providing specific information about ethnic heritage.[3] Students whose responses to the survey yielded data indicating biracial/ethnic heritage or identity were subsequently recruited through a flyer; students noting monoracial or multiracial (three or more) backgrounds were not approached.[4]

In order to explore questions of identity among students of different ages and from a wide range of backgrounds (ethnoracial, regional, socioeconomic, etc.), I needed a methodology capable of accommodating such diversity.[5] In-depth, ethnographic interviews were conducted using an Expressive Autobiographical Interview (EAI) technique. For the purposes of this study, the EAI probes were developed to evoke information about the participant's life history and their experiences related to ethnic identity, racial identity, and schooling contexts (Appendix C).[6] The EAI probes correspond to three interrelated domains: Social Context; Self; and Ethnic/Racial Identity. Initial interviews led to the development of eighteen new probes, and most subjects were introduced to all of the probes in follow-up interviews.

After the EAI probes were completed, a series of visuals was presented to each participant (Figures 1.1–1.4). Inspired by Gloria Anzaldúa's borderland theory as discussed by Maria Root, the visuals represent four possible modes of "experiencing, negotiating, and reconstructing the borders between races" (1996). The actual border-negotiation visuals shown are my own renderings of these concepts. These stick-figures depict four strategies for relating to different communities of heritage: Home Base/Visitor's Base; Both Feet in Both Worlds; Life on the Border; and Shifting Identity Gears.[7]

OVERVIEW OF THE STUDENTS

The survey was administered to a general population of 252 students at one public high school and one private university in the San Francisco Bay Area. Located in the heart of a community best described as having both urban and suburban features, Groveland High School is one of five district high schools serving students from socioeconomic and ethnically diverse backgrounds. Groveland is a four-year comprehensive high school with close to 1,500 students, of whom approximately 60 percent are from "minority" group backgrounds. Nearly thirty languages are spoken at Groveland, and over one-quarter of the language minority students are in NEP/LEP (non-English proficient/Limited English proficient) programs.

Groveland has been engaged in a major restructuring effort for a number of years and has introduced innovative academic programming and class scheduling. Groveland High School was ultimately chosen for its ethnically diverse population. Data collected from the school's 1996–1997 School Accountability Report Card (SARC) reveals the following student demographics: 4 percent African American; 6 percent Asian American; 51 percent Latino American; and 39 percent European American. No students of Native American Indian ancestry were noted.[8] There were 176 students enrolled in general level or advanced placement level courses in literature, language, and science at Groveland that were surveyed in this study.

Figure 1.1
Home Base/Visitor's Base

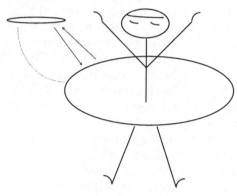

Figure 1.2
Both Feet in Both Worlds

Lakeside University is a private institution located in a suburban community in the San Francisco Bay Area. Of the approximately 6,500 undergraduates at Lakeside, the University reports
a student body that is 8 percent African American, 24 percent Asian
American, 11 percent Latino American, 2 percent Native American Indian, 51 percent European–European American, and 5 percent "Other." Demographic data for graduate students were not
available for the year. Of the students attending Lakeside University, 95 percent are from the United States. Seventy-six students
at Lakeside University were interviewed; these students were enrolled in an undergraduate/graduate or graduate level course in
the humanities, sociology, or education.

Of the 252 individuals surveyed, 63 (or 25 percent) of all respondents identified as having mixed heritage (Table 1.1). This breaks

Figure 1.3
Life on the Border

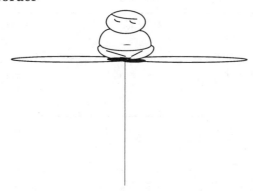

Figure 1.4
Shifting Identity Gears

down to 26 percent at the high school level and 22 percent at the university level identifying as having multiple heritage. Most of the self-identified mixed heritage students are of biracial/ethnic backgrounds (71 percent), while the rest are of multiracial heritage. It is not possible to determine by the survey whether these students were of recent (first, second, or third generation) or more distant mixed heritage.[9]

The fifteen subjects who participated in this study come from a wide range of ethnoracial backgrounds. Unless noted otherwise, the students are predominantly first generation of majority/minority (i.e., white or of color) biracial heritage, and range in age from fifteen to thirty. The following list provides a breakdown of the students by interracial ancestry. I have attempted to retain the ethnic styles of the subjects' names through the pseudonyms used in this book.[10]

Table 1.1
Percentage of Monoracial/Multiracial Students by School Level

School Level	Self-Identified Monoracial	Self-Identified Bi/Multiracial
Groveland High School	74%	26%
Lakeside University	78%	22%

Majority/Minority Biracial Heritage	*Name and Age*
African American and European American	Alex Bell, 16
	Kris Dawson, 21
	Steve Billings, 15
Asian and European American	Kay Meki, 25
East Indian–Middle Eastern and European American	Jocelyn Saghal, 28
	Prakash Moghadam, 24
	Sandy Zubaida, 21
Latino–Latino American and European American	Marta Elizondo, 30
	Melanie Newheim, 16[11]
	Donna Tesh, 21
Native American Indian and European American	Missy Connor, 15
	Karen Loomis, 17[12]
	Sheila Rafkin, 17
Asian American–Latino American	Yvonne Garcia, 21
Afro-Caribbean–Asian American	Amanda Wilson, 21

The students represent a variety of geographic, socioeconomic, and community backgrounds (Table 1.2). All but two students were born in the United States, and each were raised in the United States since their early years. Six students have at least one foreign-born parent, and one has both foreign-born parents, reflecting the changing immigration patterns since the 1960s. Based on students' descriptions of their parents' occupations since birth, parents' educational background, and stories about family experiences, seven students can be described as coming from middle to upper-middle-class backgrounds and eight from lower-middle to lower-class backgrounds.

In terms of the ethnic and racial diversity of the communities in which they were raised, five students describe growing up in predominantly white or mainstream communities and five say they

Table 1.6
Student Demographics

Student	Place of Birth	Foreign Born Parent(s)	Family Socio-economic Status	Community Demographics
Alex Bell*	California	none	lower	mixed and white
Steve Billings*	California	none	lower	mixed
Missy Connor*	California	none	lower	mixed
Kris Dawson*	Michigan	none	lower	white
Marta Elizondo	California	none	lower	white
Yvonne Garcia*	Mexico	father	lower	mixed and minority
Karen Loomis	California	none	middle	mixed
Kay Meki	Missouri	father	middle	white
Prakash Moghadam	Illinois	father	upper middle	white
Melanie Newheim	California	none	middle	mixed
Sheila Rafkin	California	none	lower middle	mixed
Jocelyn Saghal	California	mother/father	middle	mixed and white
Donna Tesh	Washington	mother	upper middle	white
Amanda Wilson	New York	father	lower middle	minority
Sandy Zubaida	Iran	father	upper middle	white

*Indicates parents are divorced.

are from ethnoracially mixed communities bordered by mainstream neighborhoods. Only two students noted they were raised in predominantly minority community contexts (Mexican–Mexican American and Asian–Asian American). Three students describe transitioning between predominantly white and mixed communities during their childhood and teenage years. Finally, in all fifteen cases, students' parents were married at some point, although two-thirds of the parents are currently married. The student portraits that follow provide more detailed biographies of each student.

STUDENT PORTRAITS

Alex Bell

Alex Bell is a sixteen-year-old junior attending Groveland High School. His mother, who is European American, is from northern California and works as a house cleaner; his father, who is African American, is from New York and works as a municipal services

employee. They also have an older son. Alex's parents divorced when
he was six and they now live a few miles apart. When Alex was nine,
his mother remarried and they moved from Excelsior into some predominantly white suburban communities over the course of three years.
Because of the racism he faced in the suburbs, Alex returned to live
with his father in Excelsior when he was twelve. His mother soon
followed, and Alex often stays with her on the weekends.

Tall with pale olive skin, a full smile, and a head of dark wavy
hair, Alex slides easily back and forth between standard and black
English as we speak. As he explains, speaking black English is a
sign of respect, or of being comfortable with his interlocutor. He
says both his parents have instilled in him a strong sense of pride
in his linguistic and ethnoracial heritage. While he feels most people
see him as black, Alex also says that he simultaneously is seen as
mixed because of his very fair skin. Alex generally identifies as
mixed, both black and white, and never just white. Yet he also defines himself generally as culturally black because, he says, "that's
the way I've grown up."

Steve Billings

Steve Billings is a fifteen-year-old freshman at Groveland High
School. His father, who is African American, is a retired Vietnam
veteran and is disabled. His mother, who is European American,
works as a secretary. Steve's parents divorced when he was seven
and he now lives with his mother in Excelsior, his birthplace. Lately
Steve has been able to visit his father, who lives about an hour
away, once every month.

With his light tan complexion, hazel eyes, caramel-colored hair,
and ambiguous features, Steve says most people assume he's white
until they learn about his mixed heritage. Adding a twist to his
response on the survey I administered, Steve recently found out
his father is also part Arapaho Indian. Steve consistently identifies as mixed, both black and white (and sometimes Arapaho), and
never just one heritage, stating that this is just what he is and how
he chooses to represent himself.

Missy Connor

Born and reared in the diverse community of Excelsior for most
of her life, Missy Connor is a fifteen-year-old sophomore at
Groveland High School. Missy's mother, who is European American, is from northern California and works as a school secretary.
Missy's father is a Native American Indian from Ohio who met her

mother through relatives while visiting California. Missy's parents divorced when she was in the fifth grade, and her father returned to Ohio. Her mother soon married a Portuguese American man who works as a mechanic and engineer, and they moved to a nearby community four years ago. Missy has one younger sister, but pointed out that her mother's brother also married someone who is Native American, so she has a cousin of similar mixed heritage. Although her sister maintains contact, Missy is not in touch with her father and therefore cannot say what type of work he does.

Generally seen as white, Missy is quick to note that her light skin, blond hair, and dark brown eyes attract regular comments from strangers who do not expect a blond to have dark eyes. Missy often struggles to make her Indian heritage known, especially when socializing in minority contexts where she is assumed to be a "white girl." In these contexts, Missy says she finds herself changing how she talks even though she's a native speaker of standard English. When asked about her heritage, Missy says she responds by saying she's half Indian and half white, never just one or the other. Missy stresses the fact that she is not Indian, which she equates with being "full," and describes her recent discomfort at receiving a monthly subsidy from the government. As she explains, she feels "they were saying that I'm, like, full Indian but I wasn't. I didn't feel like taking their money even though . . . they kind of explained it in the letter. . . . Then my aunt, [who] is full Indian . . . explained it to me more."

Kris Dawson

Kris is twenty-two years old and in her fourth year of undergraduate work at Lakeside University. Born in Trent, Michigan, to a European American mother and an African American father, Kris has had a complicated life, and her story is difficult to profile. I will try to do so here with care. Her mother was working as a secretary after receiving her B.A. in French and History when she married Kris's father, who has always been independently employed. When Kris was about two, her mother took her and her older sister out to suburban Seattle, Washington. There, while Kris's mother continued to work as a secretary, they moved several times within generally affluent and predominantly white communities. During this time, her mother effectively cut ties with all relatives in the Midwest, although Kris's father and his relatives did visit them in Washington. Kris does not recall her father's visits with fondness.

When she was seven, her father came to Seattle to take Kris and her sister for a week-long trip to the beach. Her father ended up abducting them and taking them to live in Mexico for two years. He later brought them back to their mother, who then moved the girls again, and all three underwent permanent name changes. Kris has had no contact with her father since that time. Kris dropped out of middle school when her home life was especially difficult and, after some hospitalization, enrolled in an alternative high school. After taking a while to finish high school, Kris was encouraged by a counselor to apply for college, although she was more interested in working. After a few years at a community college, Kris enrolled at Lakeside University. She says her relationships with her older sister and her mother (who now works as a network administrator for a large company) have improved in the past few years.

Growing up with her mother and in predominantly white communities, Kris says that during her childhood she would alternate between wanting to be just black or just white. In the past, Kris describes unconsciously sliding into black English when spending time with her few black peers, although she says she becomes aware of her style shifting and reverts back to a more mainstream standard English. Kris overtly describes struggling with negative societal stereotypes about blacks and says she has consciously tried to emphasize her whiteness to outsiders. Yet, Kris identifies herself culturally as more white than black not only because of her preferences, but also because of her ethnic experiences. At the time of these interviews, Kris said she's just recently become more comfortable identifying "half-and-half," and sees herself in some contexts as feeling more black identified in positive ways, while in others settings definitely feeling more white.

Marta Elizondo

Marta is a thirty-year-old master's student at Lakeside University, which she also attended as an undergraduate. Her father is second-generation Mexican American and grew up in Texas and California, while her mother is a second-generation Italian American and German American from Oregon. Her mother works as a school secretary; and her father, who for many years worked as a carpenter, recently received his contractor's license. After living in a predominantly Mexican–Mexican American part of San Jose, California until Marta was seven, her family moved to a largely German American suburb of Portland, Oregon. There, she and her four siblings attended private schools on scholarship where they often were the only students of Mexican heritage. Before her senior year in high school, Marta's family moved back to their current home of San Jose where, she explains, for the first time she was encouraged to apply to college by a school counselor.

Marta learned Spanish in high school, but says she does unconsciously slip into a Chicano dialect in certain contexts even though it was not an intimate part of her background. Her lack of a regional accent when she speaks Spanish, she says, conspires with her green eyes, white skin, and dark brown hair to encourage outsiders to question her heritage. Although Marta strongly identifies as culturally Chicana or Mexican American (since this was the dominant home culture), her identification changes and she will also describe herself as a mixed-race Latina because she feels she is often suspected of not being "full."

Yvonne Garcia

Yvonne is a twenty-one-year-old senior who is graduating from Lakeside University. She was born in Tijuana, Mexico, although at the time her family technically lived across the border in San Diego. Yvonne's father, who is Mexican, is from the Tijuana area and has many relatives there. He has worked as a valet and has held several different positions within the catering industry. Yvonne's mother is from Hawaii and is Japanese American. She was a hairstylist when she moved to California, and has worked as a companion for the elderly, a school aide, and community liaison. They met when he was working as a valet for the building where Yvonne's mother lived. Yvonne's two siblings, an older brother and a younger sister, were both born in Tijuana as well, where her parents lived for a while early in their marriage. Yvonne lived in East San Diego until her parents divorced when she was three. She then moved with her mother and brother to Hawaii for two years, where she attended preschool and kindergarten. When they returned to California, Yvonne's parents reunited and they lived in South San Diego, where she grew up until she left for college.

Living in a predominantly Mexican–Mexican American part of town, Yvonne says her mother adopted the local culture. She and her siblings were raised in the Catholic church and spent a lot of time with their father's family in Tijuana. Her parents separated permanently when Yvonne was about ten, and she has had little contact with her father since coming to college. Her mother moved to Hawaii around this time as well, where she is taking care of her aging parents. Yvonne recalls her elementary magnet school as being more diverse that her junior and senior high school experiences. These latter institutions, she says, were overwhelmingly

Mexican, Mexican American, and Filipino, with only a handful of whites and blacks. (Yvonne did attend a private preparatory high school for a few months on full scholarship; however, the affluence and lack of diversity made her feel uncomfortable, so she opted to drop out and attend her neighborhood high school.) Since her mother did not speak Spanish, however, Yvonne describes feeling different from her peers, the majority of whom spoke Spanish in the home. This difference, however, was exacerbated by her physical appearance and often led her peers to question her Mexicanness.

Yvonne agrees that most people see her as someone of Asian descent. Her almond-shaped eyes, straight hair, and very pale skin lead many to assume she is Chinese or Japanese, she says. But Yvonne points out that her light brown eyes and light brown hair contrasts with these other features and encourage people to make comments about her appearance and inquire about her heritage. (Recently, Yvonne's taken to dyeing her hair dark, which she says is more of a "match" with her other features.) Yvonne strongly identifies Mexican American or Chicana, although since coming to college she's been more willing to identify as both Japanese and Mexican on surveys if she feels it is important to mention. In person, Yvonne responds by saying she is half Mexican and half Japanese because she feels that people "want to know both," noting with frustration how people never believe that she is Mexican. This contrast between her physical appearance and her ethnic identity does not pose a conflict for Yvonne, who says some people have asked if she feels "bad" about giving preference to her Mexican heritage over her Japanese heritage. She says "I don't, 'cause I don't have that experience. I don't know what it feels like to be Asian American in the United States, because I haven't had that experience."

Karen Loomis

Karen is an eighteen-year-old senior at Groveland High School, and like many of her peers in this study, she was born and raised in Excelsior. Karen is of third generation mixed heritage. Her mother, who has worked as a bank teller for many years, is from New York and of Irish, French, and English heritage. As long as she can remember, her father has worked for a water bottling company, briefly as a manager and mostly as a truck driver. Raised in California, Karen's father is half Native American Indian and half white. Karen is an only child, but does have two half-brothers from her father's first marriage.

Having light brown eyes, curly brown hair, and fair skin, Karen explains, she is usually seen as a "white person." She says her connection to her American Indian heritage has been through her father's relatives, especially her late grandfather who lived close by when she was very young. When she was in third grade, Karen's family took a road trip to Oklahoma for a family reunion and there, she says, she learned more about her relatives on this side of the family. It was at this time that Karen was registered as a member of several groups, although she is unsure about her exact tribal affiliations and refers to Creek, Cherokee, and Choctaw. Karen has attended several local pow wows, and recalls fondly attending one with her grandfather and friend (who is also part Native American and part white) when she was very young. Karen says otherwise, her experiences have been pretty much like her mainstream European American peers.

In terms of her identification, Karen says she is proud of her Native American heritage and enjoys responding to surveys so she can express this side of her ancestry. Karen contends "I guess I'm proud of being American Indian. . . . It's not like . . . I'm half. But even though I'm an eighth it's better than none at all. And so I'm proud of it because not everybody can be Native American." Karen does not like having to choose one heritage over the other and if forced to pick, she says she would choose to represent herself as a Native American rather than white seemingly because it's more interesting, or as she explains, it "doesn't seem like there's many Native Americans around as there used to be and I like to just show what I have."

Kay Meki

Kay Meki is a twenty-two-year-old master's student at Lakeside University. Kay's mother, who is European American, holds a master's degree in linguistics; and her father, who is Japanese, works as an engineer. Her parents met at college in St. Louis, Missouri, where Kay was later born. When she was young, Kay's family moved to a Northern California suburb near Lakeside where (except for a few years living in Virginia during her elementary and initial junior high school years) she and her two sisters grew up. Kay says she began to have more Asian American classmates in junior high school in Northern California, where she later found a strong Japanese American community.

When she was younger, Kay explains, people would ask her if she was Native American, Hawaiian, or Chicana–Mexican. In conjunction with her ethnically vague surname, Kay's light brown hair, white skin, freckles and almond eyes seem to contribute to her ambiguity to outsiders. She says that as the Hapa, or part Asian, part white, community continues to grow in Northern California, she is more recently being asked if she is part Asian. And Kay will change her identification depending upon the intention of the inquirer. Generally, Kay identifies as "Nikkei," a word that means "of Japanese descent" and can encompass her mixed heritage. At times, she will be specific and say "Nikkei America-jinn," which means of Japanese descent but from America. Kay also says that in certain contexts she is safe to identify as Japanese and white, but because of the politics and ignorance surrounding race and mixed heritage, she usually is not afforded the "luxury really fully being that."

Prakash Moghadam

Prakash Moghadam is a twenty-four-year-old master's student at Lakeside University. His mother is Croatian and German American (third generation on both sides) and works as a nurse and bookkeeper in her husband's medical office. Prakash's father is East Indian and is a medical doctor. He came to the United States in 1954 and met Prakash's mother in Pennsylvania, where she was born and raised. They have three children together, Prakash's two younger sisters, and they do not speak any of their father's languages.

Prakash was born and raised outside Chicago, where there is an established Indian community in which the family participates. While his parents' relatives were geographically distant, Prakash says they did grow up visiting his Croatian cousin in Chicago quite regularly. His mother is a practicing Catholic and his father is a practicing Hindu, yet they did not pressure their children to choose one religion or attend services with them. However, Prakash does feel his mother adopted the Indian community and, therefore, their Indian heritage was especially stressed in the home. He describes his family as often participating in both professional and social Indian organizations, and describes his sisters as being very active in various cultural and political groups.

Prakash identifies ethnically as Indian, and yet generally with all of his heritage. On forms, he will rebel against mutually exclusive categories and write in "other—Indian and Croatian–German," although at other times he will mark Asian if that is available. When asked how he responds to questions about his heritage in person, Prakash explains that he'll say (half) Indian and (half) Croatian and German. With his white skin, more European features, and dark hair and eyes, he says he usually puts Indian first for two reasons: first, because that is what people are trying to verify in light of his name and ambiguous features; and second, because he identifies more with this side of his heritage.

Melanie Newheim

Melanie is a junior who attends Groveland High School. She was born and raised around the Excelsior area, as were her father and mother, who initially met and began dating when they attended Groveland. Her parents divorced when she was three, and both remarried soon after. Melanie has one older full brother, and two younger half brothers from her mother's second marriage. Her mother works as a secretary, although earlier she did work at home taking care of Melanie's younger brother, who has cerebral palsy. Melanie's father, who works as a truck driver, moved to Utah when she was in the eighth grade and is of German American heritage. Melanie's stepfather works as a mechanic and is of Norwegian American ancestry.

Melanie is of second generation mixed heritage, and all of her grandparents live in Excelsior. She notes that her father's mother, who is German American, has recently shown an interest in teaching Melanie about her German heritage. On the other side of the family, Melanie's Hispanic heritage is more difficult to detail. Melanie alternately refers to her mother as half German American (or white) and half Spanish (or Hispanic or Mexican). Her grandfather on this side has relatives in New Mexico, and possibly in Mexico. Reviewing Melanie's interview, I found several references to eating Mexican foods at her grandparents' house, as well as the term Mexican being used interchangeably with Spanish. So I suspect the family prefers the term Spanish over Mexican to denote their Hispanic heritage.

Melanie describes learning a little about her Spanish–Mexican background from trips to New Mexico and spending time with her grandfather; she also studied Spanish for a while. She says her family regularly meets to share a big Sunday dinner at her grandparents' house, where her German American grandmother learned how to prepare Mexican food from her mother-in-law. At these times, Melanie says she feel the most connected to her Hispanic ancestry. Melanie feels that "even though I have . . . a quarter Hispanic in me . . . it's not recognized. And I don't even really know that much about it. It's like 'Oh, yeah, I used to go down to Mexico and visit all [of] my grandparents' relatives . . . and they showed me how to make food and stuff. [But] people . . . I don't know. They don't really think of me like that . . . 'cause I'm so white-looking." With hazel eyes, dark blond hair, and very fair skin, Melanie says she is viewed by others as white, a term she sees as offensive in the Excelsior context where white students are in the minority at Groveland. For this reason, on forms Melanie alternates between checking both (even if this is not allowed) and putting nothing at all. In person, Melanie says she now identifies as "75 percent European American and 25 percent Hispanic."

Sheila Rafkin

A senior at Excelsior High School, Sheila was born and raised in Redwood City and is eighteen years old. She has one older and one younger brother. Sheila describes her mother, who is third generation Irish American, as a Southern Californian from an upper middle class background. She has worked for many years as a secretary, and recently became a legal secretary. Sheila says her father works as a courier and has held several different blue collar jobs since she was born (with the post office, a garage door company, a gas station, and the sheriff's department). She describes him as a "full blood" Chippewa who was raised on a reservation in Minnesota, where he left high school early to join the marines. Sheila's father met her mother there at a party when he was traveling for a lecture series after returning from the Vietnam War. Over the course of her life, Sheila has had one occasion to meet a relative on her father's side, when her grandmother came to live with her family for a while when she was young. Her most frequent connections to relatives are with her mother's side of the family in southern California; she says her grandparents recently have talked at length about her Irish ancestors, their immigration, and their experiences in the United States.

Sheila has brown eyes, long dark brown hair, and pale olive skin, although she notes she is much darker than her mother, who has red hair, freckles, and very pale skin. Attending school in the Bay Area, Sheila says she is mostly seen as white and sometimes asked if she is Latina or Mexican. Sheila identifies as both Chippewa, or Native American, and Irish American, and says she relates to both of her ancestries through their common experiences with oppression. Sheila is opposed to having to choose one heritage over another on official forms or test, and says "I feel that it eliminates the other half of me, [like] I'm being asked to cut off my other arm. . . . They always talk about your self-confidence . . . but if you have to identify only half of yourself, then it's going against everything people have been talking about."

Jocelyn Saghal

Jocelyn is a twenty-eight-year-old master's student at Lakeside University. She was born in Hollywood, California, where her parents met at a party, and she has one younger brother. Her mother, who is Swiss, holds a B.A. and was working for a film producer at the time while her father, who is East Indian, was working on his Ph.D. in civil engineering. Her father's work took the family around the world and, in fact, Jocelyn moved once or twice a year for the first thirteen years of her life. Before the age of five, Jocelyn moved around southern and northern California several times. When she was five, they moved to Australia for two years, then to Tanzania, Africa, for two years. At this time, her mother took Jocelyn and her brother to live in Switzerland before reuniting with her husband in Southern California when Jocelyn entered the third grade. The family then moved to Florida, where Jocelyn was bussed to a predominantly black school for the fourth grade, then enrolled in a private Christian school in the fifth grade. Her sixth grade year was split between Albuquerque, New Mexico, and Washington state. Finally, in seventh grade Jocelyn attended school in Florida for about five months, and then her family moved and settled in Southern California that same year. After moving to a different middle school, Jocelyn completed all of her high school work at one institution, and then did her undergraduate work at UC Santa Cruz. Although she is currently a homemaker, before Jocelyn attended college, her mother worked as a translator, a bank employee, and in retail at various points.

With multilingual and international parents, Jocelyn explains that English was the common language of the household; she does not speak German, French, Punjabi, or Hindi, although her brother majored in German and currently lives in Switzerland. Jocelyn feels her parents wanted their children to be Americans, so no single culture was stressed more than the other in their home. Jocelyn has medium-dark skin, black wavy hair, dark eyes, and narrow features that, combined with her name, encourage people to ask about her heritage. Although she sees herself as American and Swiss and Indian, Jocelyn feels that saying she's "mixed" can be too vague. So when asked how she identifies, Jocelyn responds by saying she's from here (the United States), her father is from India and her mother is from Switzerland, and lets others try to figure out what that means in terms of her ethnic and racial identity.

Donna Tesh

Donna Tesh is a twenty-one-year-old master's student attending Lakeside University. She also attended Lakeside as an undergraduate, where her father's family represents several generations of Lakeside alumni. Donna was raised in a predominantly white, affluent suburb in the Northwest. Donna's parents only recently divorced. Her mother, who is a Latinegra woman from Panamá, has held many white collar jobs and now works for a state agency; she began, although did not complete, her Ph.D. work. Her father, who is Dutch American, works as a fishery marine biologist and holds an M.A.

Donna has light olive skin, blue eyes, light-brown and blond kinky hair, and ambiguous features. Her experiences as a woman of color in predominantly white settings, she says, preclude her from wanting to, let alone being able to, identify as white. Although her mother is a Latina, Donna finds herself drawn to the African American community because of her racial heritage. In her interviews, Donna eloquently details how she is perceived as a black woman in a white society, but somehow not quite black enough in the black community. She notes that she has been unsuccessful speaking black English, pointing out that it is not a part of her background. Donna is regularly questioned about her heritage as people are curious and want to determine her parentage. She says that being from a mixed background means she has to "make a choice . . . [in] the way I talk, walk, act around others, [and] choose to live my life. . . . Also, I have to deal with people around me in public . . . how they see me . . . and I think that has to do with people on the outside looking in." Therefore, Donna identifies mostly as a mixed-race black woman, often as black, and never just white.

Amanda Wilson

Amanda Wilson is a twenty-two-year-old master's student at Lakeside University. Amanda grew up in Brooklyn, New York, and only recently moved out to California for her graduate work. Amanda's mother, who is second generation Chinese American, was born and raised in New York City's Chinatown. She met Amanda's father, who is an Afro-Jamaican, through mutual friends when he was visiting New York City on vacation. After several years of courtship via the mail, her parents married and had Amanda and her older brother. Amanda's father has worked as a carpenter and recently received his contractor's license. Her mother recently retired from a career as a high school teacher. They are married and still live in New York City. Amanda's childhood was closely connected to the Chinese American community in New York City, and her family used to visit relatives in Jamaica on an annual basis.

People see many different traits in Amanda; with her light brown skin, wavy black hair, and ambiguous features, she is seen by others as alternately African American, Hawaiian, Latina, East Indian, and Middle Eastern. Amanda consistently identifies as both Chinese and black, although she grew up strongly identifying culturally as Chinese because, she says, "We were surrounded by Chinese." She learned in elementary school, however, that her features would preclude her from being accepted as Chinese by others in the Chinese American community. A recent born-again Christian, Amanda says she relates equally "to both sides [of her heritage] by being Christian," although she says recently she has started changing her response on surveys to identify solely as black out of political concern for the African American community.

Sandy Zubaida

Recently graduated from UC Santa Barbara, Sandy is a twenty-two-year-old master's student at Lakeside University. Sandy's mother, who is Swiss American, and her father, who is Iranian, met while attending graduate school at UC Berkeley. Sandy and her older sister were born in Tehran, Iran, where they grew up bilingual speaking both Farsi and English. At the age of four, her family was forced to leave Iran because of the revolution and they resettled in northern California, where Sandy's younger brother was born. Her mother works as an ESL teacher and has a B.A. in Latino Studies and an M.A. in geography. Her father was vice chancellor of a university in Iran, and now works as a chemical engineer.

Growing up about an hour away from Lakeside, Sandy was in a majority white community for most of her life. She says her primary exposure to Persian culture came through her father's music, cooking, and television shows; otherwise, she describes her life as firmly grounded in a mainstream European American culture. While they also were involved in her mother's Catholic church, another connection to the Persian community came through the family's participation in her father's Baha'i faith, through which Sandy developed some friendships with other Persian kids during her elementary and junior high school years.

With white skin, light brown hair, and light eyes, Sandy says she is most often seen as a European American. However, her almond-shaped eyes and ambiguous last name lead people to inquire about her heritage, sometimes asking is she's Italian. Like most of the students in this study, Sandy's identification shifts depending on the context. Ultimately, she views herself as both Persian and (European) American. Although she's lost her ability to speak Farsi, Sandy most often responds to questions about her heritage by stating that she is Persian in order to help clarify her ethnic ambiguity. And yet on forms, she will identify as Caucasian or white ever since an incident in grade school when a teacher informed her that she should not choose "Asian" because she wasn't Asian, but white.

NOTES

1. Researchers are beginning to take note of these limitations. Note Cross and Fhagen-Smith (1996).

2. Ethnicity and race were treated as separate constructs.

3. The use of the race/ethnicity survey was important because it attempted to avert four typical problems associated with the recruitment of biracial/ethnic subjects. First, the survey allowed me to avoid a straight "word of mouth" or snowballing approach. Second, any potentially negative connotations of mixed heritage were played down by administering the survey among a general student population, thereby avoiding a spotlight on mixed race students. Third, for individuals who are more likely to stress ethnic over racial heritage (and who would therefore be averse to questions based solely on race), the survey incorporated both racial and ethnic terminology. And fourth, because the survey mirrored the Office of Management and Budget's (MBO's) five-race framework, data collected through the instrument would be consistent with contemporary definitions of racial and ethnic identity. Respondents were free to check as many of the categories they felt best described their racial and ethnic heritage. In addition, a sixth category for "Biracial or Multiracial Heritage" was also included. Students were given the following options: filling out information on their parents' races; providing another word to describe their mixed racial heritage; or declining to specify.

4. The flyer attempted to diminish the tendency of attracting a selective sample by emphasizing "mixed/biracial heritage" and noting self-identification was not a factor for participation. Written consent was obtained from each participant as well as from the parent or custodian of those students under the age of eighteen. High school students were paid five dollars for their participation in this study and university students were not remunerated.

5. The EAI blends a chronological life history, or autobiography, a technique with a structured expressive interview method in order to draw out the subject's view of reality as it relates to a desired topic. The interviewer develops questions around the topic and then directs these questions at the subject during crucial points of the subject's narrative account (Spindler 1987). The EAI was selected because it can concisely elicit life history information from a large number of key actors and strategically target experiences related to specific issue. The EAI probes could, therefore, accommodate fluid, dynamic, and multiply-situated identities as well as those grounded in a single reference group orientation.

6. Every participant was informed of their right to refuse a question, end the interview at any time, or choose to revoke information shared with the interviewer at any future point. Participants were also assured

that their anonymity would be maintained through the use of pseudonyms.

7. Each subject was told they would be shown four pictures describing how a person of multiple ancestry may experience their identity in relationship to their communities of heritage. The subjects were informed that none of the visuals were meant to imply a negative relationship, and that all should be viewed as positive, creative strategies. It was also stressed that participants may not find any of the pictures representative of their reality, or that one, more than one, or all of the visuals may be appropriate. The subjects were encouraged to provide feedback on the visuals, including any suggestions for changes that would make any visual more applicable to their situation.

8. No SARC was produced during the 1995–1996 academic year at Groveland, which corresponds to the year during which I recruited students for the study.

9. This project is informed by a pilot study I conducted at Groveland High School in 1994 to examine the administrative process of collecting and reporting student data based on race and ethnicity. There were three major findings. First, there existed disparities between student self-reported data of race/ethnicity and official school-reported data. Second, student, teacher, and administrator perceptions about data collection of race/ethnicity are related to their personal attitudes about cultural diversity and intergroup relations. And finally, 30 percent of the randomly surveyed students self-identified as having multiracial/cultural heritage.

10. The names of all individuals and many of the locations have been changed to pseudonyms to protect the identity of the study participants.

11. Second generation biracial.

12. Fourth generation biracial.

Chapter 2

Surveying the U.S. Racial Ecology

Common definitions of race in the United States invoke references to blood, phenotype, kinship, purity, power, and conflict. Such images are linked to what Malkki (1992) calls the modernist metaphors of space and place that shape our everyday understandings of identity, racial and otherwise. These physical and metaphysical notions of identity and belonging are central to our society's racial ecology, or the shared conceptual landscape we inhabit that provides us with a sense of orientation in relation to others (Root 1996). Like the mapping of our physical world, this cognitive landscape is parceled along boundaries that presumably demarcate the beginnings and endings of discrete racial communities (Gupta and Ferguson 1992; Malkki 1992). Even though the idea of race as a valid way of organizing humans is widely challenged today, it nonetheless remains an important construct that deeply informs public and private life in the United States (Glass and Wallace 1996; Hollinger 1995; West 1993).

The racial landscape of the United States is unique, informed by the particular struggles and identities of the different people who comprise our society's history. With roots in the religious world, racial classification systems in Western European societies during the nineteenth century were encouraged by the scientific revolution and an emergent social Darwinism (Ehrlich and Feldman 1977; Omi and Winant 1986). The scientific language of these classification systems imparted a sense of legitimacy to the process of ascribing random social attributes to different biological types, races, or subspecies of human beings. European typologies of race served to organize people within a hierarchy that ranked their perceived physical, intellectual, and moral capacities against a self-serving standard set by the privileged social groups who produced the typologies (Spickard 1992).

Racial classification systems, therefore, served an ideological function: By justifying the social order, the science of race claimed to provide "objective" proof that the given power structure was somehow preordained by nature or God. In this way, the deployment of race through social policy helped to safeguard elite centers of power from contamination or infiltration by economically, phenotypically, and culturally dissimilar groups. The evolutionary undertones of these systems neatly dovetailed with the capitalist and Protestant foundations of the Anglo United States by reinforcing an illusion that the given social order was the result of a "competition of the survival of the fittest" in which all participants competed on equal footing (Glass and Wallace 1996).

LOCATING MIXED RACE

Within this developing ecology of race, social mechanisms were necessary to address the consequences of interracial transgressions (either attempted or achieved) and maintain order in the realm of everyday life. The need for such mechanisms became even more critical for whites of various class backgrounds after the abolition of slavery. As white slaveholders lost the control to define who was free and who was enslaved via paternity laws ascribing mixed race African Americans to slave status, there was an urgency to introduce other vehicles for protecting their centers of power and privilege (Davis 1991; King and DaCosta 1996). Among some lower status whites, freed African Americans presented the threat of greater competition over already scarce resources.

In the post–Civil War United States, establishing legal consequences for miscegenation (race mixing) and formalizing the rule of hypodescent were necessary to sustain the racial hierarchy. Often referred to as the "one-drop rule," hypodescent generally applies to individuals of white–nonwhite heritage by defining them as members of the nonwhite racial group, or the most socially subordinate group in the case of minority/minority heritage.[1] The term *hypodescent* presupposes a hierarchy of race and corresponding privileges, a correlation that was uniquely consequential in the pre–Civil Rights United States. Although there has been some change over time, white Northern European American groups have been located toward the top of this hierarchy, African Americans at the bottom, and other nonwhite groups occupying varying statuses.[2] Hypodescent (herein referred to as the one-drop rule) was the default mechanism for dealing with the effects of miscegenation by preventing mixed-race individuals from claiming privilege as whites regardless of their blood quantum.

Theoretically at least, the cultivation of one-drop logic meant that mixed race individuals of part white ancestry in the pre–Civil Rights era were considered "people of color" regardless of their ethnic experience, blood quantum, or phenotype. Spickard contends that from the perspective of racialized minority groups, therefore, "race is by no means only negative. . . . From the point of view of subordinate[d] peoples, race can be a positive tool, a source of belonging, mutual help, and self-esteem" (Spickard 1992). In a society with a history of oppression and aggression toward nonwhite people, it may be safe to assume that most mixed-race individuals in the past have viewed their requisite minority status as natural, necessary, and welcome. Thus, the one-drop rule is often seen by racialized minority groups as a positive source of unity, self-actualization, and a tool for survival in an oppressive society.

While the one-drop rule is an unspoken standard that is accepted by communities of color, the ascription of mixed race members is not without tension. For example, in the African American community there are longstanding issues around skin tone and physical characteristics. Discrimination favoring European skin tones (colorism) and features (featurism) is exacerbated by the group's history with "passing"; that is, European-looking people of mixed descent denying their African heritage in order to acquire benefits as whites in the era of Jim Crow, in particular.[3] The community's experiences as an oppressed group shape not only how dating, marriage, and sex between blacks and others (especially whites) are viewed. The group's shared history also impacts how recently mixed individuals are perceived and treated within the community given their status in the collective imagination as representatives of the legacy of miscegenation—as potential passers or reminders of the rape of black women by white men.

Thus, the notion that individuals belong to one community is deeply embedded in our society. Whether of the ethnic or racial type, pluralism is widely imagined in spatial terms that neatly map (literally and figuratively) communities as discontinuous spaces. In many ways, people are seen as metaphysically bound to these spaces, naturally "rooted" to one community through the fact of birth and blood (Malkki 1992). This is the primary reason we find it so difficult to toss the one-drop rule into the dustbin of history, even though we seem to be outgrowing it. Yet, Fernández (1992) suggests our inability may also stem from a pervasive uneasiness about racial transgressions:

> [The] disparate treatment of intermarriage is a direct re-
> sult of racism and racist practices of segregation and dis-
> crimination. . . . The offspring of so-called interracial
> relationships have not been accorded a distinctive iden-
> tity. . . . This failure to accommodate what are regarded as
> interracial relations and people in the United States is, at
> heart, an unresolved American identity crisis . . . and makes
> the resolution of the general race problem virtually impos-
> sible. (p. 132)

As a result of these external social conditions, Nakashima (1992) notes how mixed-heritage individuals often are expected to fit into traditional ethnic and racial identity models since there is no space for articulating a mixed race/ethnic experience. She argues that our racial ecology has been successful in fostering one-drop logic in two ways: first, through the creation of mythological, biological, sociocultural, and sociopolitical theories or stereotypes that problem-atize the experiences of mixed race individuals; and second, through the outright denial of their existence.

The labeling of mixed heritage individuals as problems is com-mon, especially in our racial imaginings. For example, "hybrid de-generacy" theory applied to mixed race people continues to resurface in the media, popular literature, and social sciences. This botani-cal theory stereotypes recently mixed people as inferior or inher-ently tormented because of their genetic or biological lineage. A common illustration of hybrid degeneracy theory can be seen in the perennial image of the "tragic mulatta/o," usually a person of mixed black–white ancestry (the two most irreconcilable social groups). The tragic mulatto is posited as a confused, irrational, and politi-cally suspect individual who symbolizes a crisis, or a breakdown, of the laws governing the natural racial order (Root 1992; Russell, Wilson, and Hall 1992).[4]

As discussed briefly in Chapter 1, the Bowen incident and the *Time* cover are good examples of such mythology surrounding mixed heritage individuals. While Bowen's heritage was demeaned, seen as unnatural and a problem to the natural order of things, the *Time* cover speaks to "hybrid vigor" theory, or the notion that "crossbreed-ing" between human races leads to smarter, stronger, or more beau-tiful (read "exotic") people. Romantic depictions of recently mixed individuals as a "model" people, or the cultural bridges in our multicultural society, are on the rise.

And yet the commodification and consumption of mixed images, especially those of women, are longstanding practices. The tragic mulatta is depicted as a desirable and accessible female because she lies at the threshold between communities. Suspended between the mainstream ideal of white womanhood and the devalued image of black womanhood, the tragic mulatta approximates the paragon of femininity, virtue, beauty, and civilization, while representing nature, licentiousness, and things uncivilized (Streeter 1996).[5] More recently, one can look to the editorial accompanying the computer-generated *Time* image for these positive stereotypes. As the creators of this multiracial visage note, they sought to create this new "Eve" out of a composite of models from diverse ethnoracial backgrounds. After some accidents in their high-tech laboratory (note the hybrid-degeneracy theory here) which produced unsightly, cross-sexual images, the technicians fell in love with their final result, the imaginary woman whose fine features, straight hair, and slightly tanned shoulders grace the cover of the magazine. Whether positive or negative, such images reveal how contemporary representations of mixed race people continue to be informed by the stereotypes of miscegenation and mixed heritage that are deeply embedded within our racial ecology.

UNRAVELING ETHNIC AND RACIAL IDENTITY

Trying out and establishing a social identity is one of the primary features of adolescence. The development of a cohesive ethnic and racial identity can be an important part of this work, but what exactly is ethnic or racial about a person's social identity? Although the advent of popular multiculturalism has encouraged the terms to be used interchangeably (Brandt 1994; Roseberry 1992), race and ethnicity are fundamentally different. The following section attempts to unpack these concepts to show how they differ and how they inform one another.

Ethnic Identity

Ethnic identity is the dimension of a person's overall self-concept, or sense of self, that develops out of an understanding of one's membership within a particular ethnic group, and the meaning that this membership conveys (Phinney 1992, 1995). An ethnic group differs from other types of cultural groups in that the members share a sense of diffuse ancestry usually based on common geographic or national origins. Membership within the ethnic group (ethnicity) is partly ascribed, or assigned, by others based on a person's ancestry and sometimes phenotype (physical characteristics). Yet one's ethnic identity is influenced by a person's participation within a particular cultural and linguistic community (Burkey 1978). Thus, the formation of ethnic identity is a process that involves both recognition by the group and by the individual. Unlike racial identity, ethnic identity stems out of the shared cultural elements (such as values, beliefs, behaviors, mental associations, ways of speaking, traditions, etc.) which are shared by a group with a common geographic and/or religious heritage. These elements comprise, in part, the cultural models or frames of reference that guide members' interactions within the world.

The role phenotype plays in the ascription of ethnic group membership reveals the importance of race in the ethnic identity development process. Phenotype, or a person's physical appearance, can take precedence over the cultural elements of a person's ethnic identity in the ascription of ethnic group membership. The weight accorded to phenotype is especially prominent in racially segregated societies. Since a person's ethnic identity is grounded in his or her cultural experience as well, an individual may identify with an ethnic group in which they are not wholly recognized as a member due to their physical appearance. Jean Phinney (1992) helped to clarify this point by distinguishing between a person's ethnic ancestry (i.e., ethnicity) and his or her ethnic identity, underscoring how ethnic identity formation is a process that flows in both directions.

Race informs ethnic identity differently across social groups, depending largely upon a group's relative position within the racial hierarchy. In the Unites States, entrance into the sociopolitical and economic mainstream has required muting one's ethnic markers for those who differ from the Anglo-Saxon Protestant tradition. Mary Waters (1990) argues that, historically, European groups have had greater economic mobility and access into mainstream Anglo society when prominent linguistic and cultural barriers are surmounted after a few generations. Still, the mainstream is seen as devoid of any ethnic markers by mainstream white ethnics, who have the privilege of viewing ethnicity as an optional aspect of their social identities. When compared to white ethnics, nonwhite ethnic groups as a whole have not experienced comparable social mobility regardless of their length of time in the United States. Racialized minorities are not afforded the luxury of ethnically opting out, revealing the importance of how processes of racialization are different across the racial hierarchy. Simply put, to be of color is to be marked ethnic; to experience whiteness is to be unmarked by ethnicity and even race.

However, this tendency for mainstream whites to view recently arrived immigrants and people of color as essentially ethnic does not mean that their own experiences are lacking ethnic markers. Spindler and Spindler (1990) note how mainstream U.S. society is distinctly ethnic, with clear roots in Anglo-European cultures (Gay 1997). Nonetheless, as white ethnics intermarry and clear attachments to specific communities weaken, the perception remains that they have evolved beyond ethnic markers, what David Hollinger (1995) refers to as a "post-ethnic" approach toward ethnic identity. The decline in the salience of ethnicity within the personal and social lives of whites also is seen by Omi and Winant as a "racializing pan-ethnicity as 'Euro-Americans'" (McCarthy and Crichlow 1993).

James Gee's work on Discourses helps to illustrate the relationship between identity formation and community participation, which is imperative when considering the nature of ethnic identity development. Gee (1992) defines a Discourse as a web of common knowledge, mental associations, and displays recognized by group of people with similar "interests, goals and activities" (p. 107).[6] The particular Discourse communities in which we interact influence us in subtle yet profound ways: what is valued, how a value is expressed, or what and when something is worn, spoken, or done. Discourses make our behavior intelligible and meaningful to others within the community by providing a common framework for interaction, maintaining group boundaries in the process by rejecting people who stray from its course. This does not mean that Discourses are finite or inflexible; in fact, they overlap and are incomplete, malleable, and subject to disruption, although they tend to resist change from within.

Gee's distinction between acquired and learned Discourses is a critical one. An individual acquires and masters his or her primary Discourse as a child through processes of enculturation within the family and local community. Such acquisition is an unconscious process as the child engages in the social practices of the community, which provides a natural context for apprenticeship and mastery of the Discourse over a sustained period of time (Lave and Wenger 1991). While the formation of our social identities stems from our participation within Discourse communities, the primary Discourse community establishes our core social identity that will accept or challenge secondary Discourses (Gee 1992, p. 108). Gee notes that an individual may be exposed to multiple primary Discourses (which may conflict), or very little of any. A secondary Discourse is one that is consciously learned at a later age, outside the home in public spheres such as schools, churches, and other social organizations.

In these contexts where mastery of an institutionally dominant Discourse is necessary for success, individuals from nondominant Discourse backgrounds will be at a disadvantage when expected to display the appropriate codes. Individuals who are apprenticed within the dominant Discourse community are able to perform successful knowledge displays because the codes they acquired as children have become second nature to them. But for individuals who are apprenticed outside the dominant community, successful displays prove more difficult because they have learned the more obvious features, or meta-level knowledge, of the Discourse (Gee 1990, p. 117).

Gee's Discourse theory has many applications to the study of identity among recently mixed heritage people. First, it helps to better contextualize students' ethnic experiences as reflecting a single Discourse community, multiple Discourse communities, or something in-between. Were there opportunities for apprenticeship in one or both heritage communities, did these shift over time and why? Second, it allows for a consideration of the role of Discourse acquisition versus learning within the ethnic-identity development process. What are the ramifications of learning the cultural codes at a later age versus acquiring them since birth on how a person sees herself in relation to a heritage community and how she is seen by that community? And third, it provides a frame for considering how cognition and identity may be shaped by the degree of participation a mixed heritage person has within their heritage communities.

Racial Identity

Racial identity refers to the dimension of a person's overall self-concept that is grounded in his or her experiences as a member of broad racial group. The concepts of race and ethnicity are often collapsed out of confusion or for conceptual ease, but they are fundamentally distinct. A single racial group includes multiple ethnic groups and, traditionally, membership is ascribed by phenotype, or by genotype (racial ancestry), or both (Burkey 1978). Popular theories of racial identity development presume individuals to be members of a single racial group, and suggest there is one developmental trajectory that is both sequential and universal. Therefore, much of the research on racial identity attempts to determine the

degree to which an individual's identity culminates in the achievement of a racial self-concept that is in balance with their ascribed
group membership (Cross and Fhagen-Smith 1996).

It is imperative to note here how race, although an important
social marker of identity, has a particular history and character in
U.S. society. To this end, Omi and Winant's (1986) theory of racial
formation is useful because it moves beyond the research on racial
identity development to consider race as a socially constructed and
flexible category. Race is not simply a given, but a complex socio-
historical process in which racial categories are "created, inhabited, transformed, and destroyed," and through which our social
world becomes ordered in racialized ways. What we perceived as
physical and social differences distinguishing one racial group from
another in fact symbolize much broader historical conflicts that
reflect the interests of different groups over time.

Racial formation theory is useful to this work because it takes into
account how race gets done at the macro and microsociological levels,
how meanings of race shift over time, and how racial logic is not ex-
ecuted evenly. King and DaCosta (1992) help to further this theory by
providing a typology of the "four 'faces' of race." Approaching racial
formation theory from a social interactionist perspective, race is
something one "does," is a presentation of the racial self, is "done"
collectively, and is relational and hierarchical. In the following chapters, these four faces of race are revealed through the students' stories about learning to do race as people of mixed racial heritage.

LIMITATIONS OF PRIOR RESEARCH

The roots of earlier research on mixed heritage people can be
traced to "marginal man" theories from the early part of this century (Park 1928; Stonequist 1937). Generally, these marginality
theories defined mixed heritage people (or others who represented
border-type identities) as social outcasts with no place to call home
in U.S. society. The perseverance of these theories in contemporary research on mixed heritage can be contested on several grounds
(Root 1992). First, such research relies upon theoretical models that
presume identity (ethnic and racial) can be mapped and measured
in linear terms. Second, it presupposes that a healthy developmental trajectory culminates in a static identity. Third, identity is presumed to be naturally rooted in one reference group. Fourth, much
of this research is limited primarily to subjects of mixed black–
white heritage (the two most irreconcilable and socially disparate
groups in the U.S. racial ecology), and is therefore not able to be

generalized to other populations. And fifth, much of this work consists of psychological studies which are particularly limited in their scope and relevance because they often draw from clinical samples or subjects displaying "at-risk" behavior (Miller 1992).

Given these characteristics, much of the earlier research suggests that recently mixed heritage individuals who have ambiguous and open-ended self-identifications will exhibit social-psychological dysfunction when compared to monoracial peers. As mentioned in Chapter 1, applying the standards of single ancestry individuals to those of multiple ancestry renders problematic nontraditional ethnoracial experiences. New, more flexible models of racial identity formation are needed if we seek to create more accurate and illuminating portrayals of recently mixed people.

NEW DIRECTIONS IN RESEARCH

Since the early 1980s, a number of projects have responded to the need for more nuanced research into the nature of interracial/ethnic phenomena and mixed heritage identities. Unlike the research discussed, these contemporary projects take into account the broader sociopolitical context and utilize new research designs, nonclinical samples, and subjects from diverse backgrounds (Jacobs 1992; Hall 1992; Kitahara-Kich 1992; Thornton 1992; Stephan and Stephan 1991; Cauce et al. 1992).

Reconsidering the identity formation process among children and adults who assert a biracial/ethnic identity, a number of researchers are finding evidence that support a qualitatively different development process among these individuals due to their unique ethnoracial statuses and life stories (Jacobs 1992; Johnson 1992; Kitahara-Kich 1992). This study hopes to contribute to this growing body of literature by illustrating the dynamic nature of ethnic and racial identity among a highly diverse group of recently mixed heritage students.

NOTES

1. Its intent being to maintain the separation between "white" and "nonwhite," the rule of hypodescent and antimiscegenation laws generally were not concerned with race mixing between nonwhite groups.

2. It should be noted that white European ethnic groups have moved up through the U.S. racial hierarchy over time. Many white ethnic and religious groups experienced severe racism and discrimination upon their arrival in this country, although they were never considered as socially subordinate as African Americans.

3. For more information on the subject, see Daniel (1992).

4. See Spike Lee's *Jungle Fever*, or Lisa Jones's *Bulletproof Diva* (1993) for earlier references to the "tragic mulatto" stereotype.

5. The resulting image of the mixed black–white woman is desirous in the mainstream imagination because she is seen as sexually uninhibited, more dangerous and accessible than the white woman because she is closer to being black, and more attractive than the black woman because she is closer to being white (Streeter 1995). A powerful modern-day version of the tragic mulatta stereotype may be examined in the 1993 film *The Crying Game*, in which the racially ambiguous heroine transgresses boundaries not only of race, but also of gender and sexuality.

6. Gee (1990) defines discourse with a small "d" as "connected stretches of conversation" and Discourse with a capital "D" as a set of values, attitudes, ways of doing, and living in the world that is shared by a social network (p. 142).

Chapter 3

Out of the Borderlands: Interethnic/Interracial Families

As the rising rates of intermarriage and mixed heritage births attest, attitudes toward dating and marriage across lines of race and ethnicity have shifted in the United States over the past three decades. The country has experienced a doubling in the rate of interracial marriages since the 1970s, although it is not possible to determine the ethnoracial composition of these 49 million mixed marriages due to the limited data gathered by the U.S. Bureau of the Census (Table 3.1). But in 1992, the data show some 883,000 marriages of white–"other" race composition, 32,000 black–other race, and over 1 million Hispanic/other race. And while there were only 246,000 white–black marriages reported (a mere 0.5 percent of all marriages), this number represents a striking increase from the 65,000 white–black marriages reported in 1970.

Interracial/ethnic families are becoming an increasing presence within a social ecology that does not readily accommodate their existence. The surge in the number of interracial/ethnic families, and of mixed heritage children, complicates the U.S. racial ecology in many tangible ways. For example, the Bureau of the Census recorded one quarter of a million people who provided their own "multiracial designator" to describe their race on the 1990 census, and the "other" category grew at the fastest rate (45 percent), in part due to the growing numbers of multiracial individuals (Root 1996). Theoretically, children of part-white ancestry are to be identified (and presumably identify themselves) with their minority parent-

Table 3.1
Interracial Marriages in the U.S. by Group, 1992

Race	Race	Number
White	Black	246,000
White	"Other"	883,000
Black	"Other"	32,000
Hispanic	"Other"	1,155,000
Other races	Other races	Cannot determine

Source: A. F. Saluter. 1992. Marital Status and Living Arrangements: March 1992. In *Current Population Reports/Population Statistics*, ser. P-20, no. 468 (Washington, D.C.: U.S. Department of Commerce, Bureau of the Census), V-62.

age. Still, there are no social guidelines for classifying children born to two minority parents, or for those part-white individuals whose ethnic identity orientations are bicultural and otherwise nonsynchronous to traditional racial logic.

So just where do these families see themselves within such a color-coded, race-based society? While the spectrum of experiences and opinions about race, ethnicity, and identity may be as diverse as the composition of interracial/ethnic families themselves, the following chapter attempts to explore this question from the students' points of view. This chapter begins at home and considers the early lessons mixed heritage students learn about race, ethnic identity, and belonging within the family. Their stories clearly detail the challenges they face and how students (especially those of first descent) see their families as racially and culturally distinct from their same heritage peers. This perceived distinction encourages students to describe their families and home lives as unique, contributing to the construction of a mixed (or interracial/ethnic) frame of reference through which they view their ethnoracial heritage.

FAMILY LEGACIES: CHOICES, CONSEQUENCES, AND BORDER CROSSINGS

When talking about their families, mixed heritage students obviously do not focus exclusively on issues of race or ethnicity. However, the interracial and interethnic character of their families emerged as a salient feature in students' descriptions of their home lives and family histories. Students developed a clear sense of being different from most of their peers and their families, often cultivating a view of their parents as trailblazers on the frontiers of race and ethnicity. The family histories they share are characterized both in terms of loss as a result of their parents' choices, as well as strength gained from their multiple ethnic and racial roots.

Students invariably brought up their parents' distinct ethnic and racial backgrounds when asked to describe how their parents met. The courtship stories they shared emphasize how their parents crossed over ethnic, racial, and even national boundaries in order to be together. Interestingly, these depictions are conceptualized equally in both physical and spatial terms. Several students stressed how great geographical distances were traversed (either by the grandparents or the parents themselves) in order for their parents to meet. Prakash's story illustrates this point:

> Let's see, my dad is Indian, my mother is Croatian and German. She was born in the United States. . . . Her grandparents each came from Croatia and Germany. . . . Germany is kind of an amorphous term because the lines were divided so I don't even know if they were from Austria and Germany and . . . my father immigrated in '54 from India and they met in Philly, married, and had three of us. [Prakash Moghadam]

Prakash recounts his grandparents' migration to the United States, carefully delineating his parents' ethnoracial heritage via their nations of origin. Marta talks about a similar North American migration within her family tree:

> Well, like I said, my dad's from Texas and his family migrated back and forth for a long time before they finally ended up in San Jose. . . . My mom's from Portland and she was engaged to be married [when] her fiancée was in a car accident and died. . . . She needed to get away so [her family] sent her to San Francisco. . . . So while she was in San Francisco she got involved in a church group that my dad was also involved in so that's how they met. So . . . if I, even if I just go back to my grandparents' generation, and look at how long and how far the distance it had to take to make me . . . because my mom's father is from Italy so he came from Italy to the United States and all the way across the United States to the Portland area. . . . Then my grandparents were immigrants from Mexico into Texas. Then my dad came into San Jose. So it was a pretty long way to travel to get to me. And . . . pretty circumstantial, I guess that's the word. . . .

My mom could have been married to someone else and on
and on, the chances of me being here. [Marta Elizondo]

Like Prakash, Marta notes how theirs is a remarkable family history characterized in terms of migration, culture, and nation.

Marta and Prakash's stories might be seen as unremarkable,
however, given the immigration history of the United States. But their
stories suggest a new chapter to this history in light of their interracial emphasis. For example, the serendipitous meeting of students' parents is exaggerated by their racial difference, as Sandy's
story illustrates:

[My mom's] from the States and my dad was born in Iran
and grew up there and then he came here to do his graduate work at Berkeley and she was doing graduate work at
Berkeley [and that's how they met]. Yeah, actually my mom
was going to be all Latin American studies major and so she
was living in the International House because she thought
that would be a great way to meet Latinos. . . . The first
day she went down to the dining commons and she was
going to sit with Latinos . . . she sat down and she sat at
the Persian table, so she met my dad. [Sandy Zubaida]

Repeatedly, students stress the improbability of their parents meeting each other precisely because they are from racially (and ethnically) distinct communities. This conceptual geography of race is
reinforced by students' references to their parents as trailblazers
who break down barriers between groups. In this vignette, Sandy
suggests her white mother crossed over into "foreign" territory when
she attempted to sit with the Latino students and inadvertently
sat with the Persian students.[1] Other students describe their parents as trailblazers more overtly, as does Alex who relates how his
parents (a black man and white woman) were affected by crossing
over traditional racial boundaries:

I remember [my parents] used to talk about how hard it
was to be an interracial couple. They used to talk about
that. . . . The people they dealt with . . . they didn't have
any problems. People [they knew] understood . . . and they
were very comfortable with it. But . . . they said on a
soci[etal] level it was very different. People would ridicule
them, but they didn't talk to me about it a lot 'cause they
didn't want me to be upset, or for me to not understand, so
they wouldn't speak about that much. [Alex Bell]

Although his parents would not talk in depth about their experiences with racism, Alex became aware that it was something that they endured because of race, not ethnicity alone. Hearing about their parents' experiences with racism was another way some students came to learn about their parents' racial "distinctness" (one from another, as well as from other couples) and its social relevance.

For many students, the racism their parents faced was another way students highlighted the interracial character of their family lives. In several these cases, marrying outside of the group was viewed as an undesirable, even an intolerable, transgression by family members. The consequences the parents suffered for such a break from convention ranged from overt disapproval, subtle hostility, to temporary or even permanent estrangement from their relatives. Kris Dawson, whose parents separated when she was two, says her parents received disapproval from relatives on both sides of the family tree:

> They lived together for like six months . . . and they had known each other for about . . . a year. . . . They got married and . . . her parents were not happy. . . . My grandfather . . . refused to come to the wedding because my dad's black. And I think he ended up coming, but that was sort of an issue. [On my dad's side] some of them attended [the wedding]. . . . There were issues but I really don't know. He never talked about it much. . . . [Growing up] I think [my mom's white relatives] they were near, but I think that the black thing was a problem for most of them. . . . I know that my dad's mother babysat us, so there wasn't a problem there, I guess, as far as the kids were concerned. [Kris Dawson]

In another example, Marta is surprised at her grandfather's earlier hostility and temporary estrangement from her parents since he himself is interethnically married and experienced hostility from his wife's family:

> My grandfather [and grandmother] . . . that was . . . a mixed marriage—Italian and German. And my grandmother['s] . . . family disowned her for marrying my grandfather. . . . It's really interesting how that played out because they went through a lot of problems for the fact that they had married. . . . Then when my mom married my dad, my grandfather had a fit . . . he almost didn't come to the wedding. And I thought that was very . . . hypocritical, that he had

gone through the same thing with his marriage. . . . My
grandmother was [seen] as marrying down, they went
through a lot of problems for the fact that they had married. . . . Maybe that's why [my grandfather] was partly
against it, I don't know. That he had problems with [his
wife's] family and all that and didn't want to see the same
problems [for his daughter]. [Marta Elizondo]

Marta's comment suggests that her grandfather's disapproval of
her Mexican American father stems from the perceived lower racial status of the father (not because of his ethnicity alone), and
possibly some concern that his daughter will face some of the diffi-
culties he has as a partner in a mixed marriage. Amanda Wilson's
Chinese grandparents initiated a similar estrangement that lasted
for most of her life:

I knew [my grandparents] for like two years, because they
didn't talk to my mom after she married my [black Jamai-
can] dad. That's another story . . . yeah, that's another story.
But when they [got] reconciled, I learned a lot from them
just for the two years before they died. [Amanda Wilson]

In Jocelyn's case, tension emanated from both sides of her Swiss
and Indian family:

I know that [my Swiss grandmother] didn't approve of my
parents' marriage—the interracial thing. . . . At the beginning she was very discouraged and was not happy. . . . And I
know, also, on my father's side. . . . I asked my uncle about
this when I was in India . . . and he said "Well, we thought it
was interesting." But . . . there was this . . . underlying feeling "How could you marry outside your culture?" For Indians . . . one of the things that's very important to them is
marrying another Indian. My mom says they contend with
a lot of that. . . . It still feels, a lot of the times . . . [they're]
not totally at home at family functions. So that's an issue
for them. I see it played out. [Jocelyn Saghal]

Clearly, both racial and ethnic factors are at play in the decision to
become estranged from students' families. While the circumstances
varied, the students' comments suggest that most estrangements
were racially motivated and strong enough to sever their parents'
relationships with relatives, cutting off children from participation
within their extended families in the process.

In some families, the estrangement was overcome with time, and most notably after the arrival of the mixed heritage grandchildren. Marta's grandfather eventually had a change of heart toward her parents' relationship, and toward her father:

> So [my Italian grandfather] had a big fit when my parents got married but he did end up coming. Apparently, the way everybody perceives it [is] that my grandparents liked the five of us, we were his favorite grandkids. . . . He really got close to my dad and stuff . . . probably because my dad did the same line of work. My grandfather was like a welder and he was in construction, and my dad is a carpenter. . . . [They] probably got along really well that way and they shared the same values . . . so after he got to know my dad he was a lot more comfortable with everything. [Marta Elizondo]

Several students mentioned how the arrival of grandchildren acted as a salve to the damaged family ties. Yet reconciliation does not mean the formerly estranged relatives completely accept the mixed marriage, the outsider spouse, or even the mixed heritage grandchildren. In Marta's situation, for example, some of her mother's German–Italian American relatives have managed to only grudgingly accept her father over time:

> You know, they don't associate with him very much. And to the point where even us as kids have noticed that my dad doesn't really fit in and my uncles just don't [try to include him]. . . . The three of them will be together and the two uncles will be kind of associating and watching TV and going through all this stuff and not really associating with my dad. . . . I imagine it must be pretty uncomfortable for my dad. He tolerates it. It's my mom's family and, um, so I guess in that sense, I mean, even though it hasn't been explicit, I have definitely noted the, ok, you don't really belong here but we'll tolerate you. [Marta Elizondo]

When asked to describe the source of these estrangements and tensions, a few students say they feel their relatives' view the outsider as having a lower social status. Focusing again on Marta's family, she thinks some of her European American relatives see her mom as "marrying down," just as her grandmother was viewed:

> I don't know how the rest of my mom's family felt about it. . . . I very much hear what my grandfather thought,

but I don't know . . . what my aunts thought or anything like that. Although sometimes I get the sense from them, even now, that my dad's "lesser." That is true, actually, my uncles, my mom's brother in law, I have seen them react to my dad as "lesser." [Marta Elizondo]

By contrast, students note that another set of relatives viewed marrying outside of one's group as a positive, or even a logical progression. A number of students contend that their relatives approved of their parents' intermarriage. Kay Meki believes her relatives in Japan see her father as marrying the quintessential "American" because she is a white woman and, therefore, of more or less equal social status. Because of this stereotypical association of white European heritage and American identity, Kay says her Japanese relatives view her and her sisters as true Japanese Americans precisely because they are half white. Marta's Latino relatives have embraced her white mother in a similar fashion:

I know that from my [Mexican American] side of the family . . . everybody loved my mom and it could be the sense that my dad was marrying up, and you know my mom was just this precious jewel to my grandparents, and especially my grandfather. By default, I was . . . my grandfather's . . . little jewel. That's what they say anyway. I don't know because I was too little to remember. But he carried a picture of me in his wallet all the time. I was the only grandchild that he had [in his wallet], and I was not the first grandchild, my dad has . . . eight [siblings]. . . . But I was, like, the one. And I think that might be part of it . . . like I said, because . . . my mom was so valued. [Marta Elizondo]

Marta suspects that her parents' mixed marriage is accepted on the Mexican American side of the family because of her mother's comparatively higher ethnoracial status in U.S. society. In fact, she notes how this high esteem for her mother may have filtered down to the children in some ways.

INTERMARRIED WITH CHILDREN

In the following section, I consider students perceptions of life as an interracial and interethnic family. Not surprisingly, the families described in this study are quite diverse in their composition and experience. In some, the diverse ethnic and racial identities of the parents provide a quiet backdrop to family life. In others, the dominance of one parent's heritage sets the cultural tone for the entire family. Only a few students recall their parents providing them with overt messages about their mixed, or dual, heritage. Generally, the multiple nature of their ancestry rarely is discussed in a direct manner. Many mixed heritage students note how conversations with their siblings provide particularly critical opportunities for processing issues related to their biracial/ethnic heritage, such as reference group testing, physical ambiguity, cultural validity, and feelings of being both an insider and outsider.

External factors also play a role within mixed heritage students developing a sense of family. For example, physical dissimilarity emerges as an important factor that influences students' perceptions of family and belonging. As mixed heritage students begin to see how the diversity of skin tones and features in their families challenge society's definitions of kinship, they learn to view their interracial/ethnic family structures as "different" from the mainstream.

Talking about Ethnicity and Race

In most cases, parents infrequently discussed the multiple ethnic and racial heritage of the family with their children in a direct manner. Marta feels there was little need to talk about such things because her family was grounded fully in a Mexican American orientation:

> No, they never [talked about us being biracial/ethnic]. No, we were Mexican. I mean . . . I think that's how they brought us up. Not Mexican, Mexican American, only because . : . the foods that we ate and the traditions that we celebrated and how we celebrated some of our traditions. . . . No, my parents never talked about us being [biracial/ethnic], I don't remember ever talking about differences or diversity. [Marta Elizondo]

For Marta, the fact of her dual heritage is seen as a detail of the family's history. Yvonne's mother classified her as Mexican despite her more Asian phenotype: "I just remember my mom when she went to register [me for school], she always checked the Mexican box. And wouldn't put anything else. And I can't really remember why she did that, but I remember that specifically [Yvonne Garcia]." But even in the more bicultural households, most of the students similarly contend that ethnicity and race were woven subtly into the fabric of their everyday lives.

Thus, it is notable that when parents did talk with students about their mixed heritage, it was mostly in response to an external incident with racism or racist structures. In these situations, the parents' comments offer insights into how they see their children in terms of ethnicity and race. For example, the first time Melanie Newheim ever talked with her mother about being biracial was in response to an encounter with a race/ethnicity survey:

> I think the first time I really recognized [I was mixed] was when I was in elementary school. . . . I was filling out some form of ethnic heritage and it said "white," and then it said "Hispanic," and then the "Other" one. . . . My mom was sitting next to [me] and this was actually the first time I'd actually filled something out with her. . . . She was all "Well, what do you think, Melanie?" And I was all, "Uhh . . . maybe we should just check both of them." You know? Because I am Caucasian, or whatever, and I am Hispanic, but I'm not Caucasian and I'm not Hispanic. [Melanie Newheim]

In this case, Melanie's mother asked her to decide how she wanted to respond. By contrast, Amanda Wilson's mother provided her with a framework for understanding and describing her heritage/identity:

> Growing up . . . I went to elementary school in Chinatown, so like ninety percent of the kids were Chinese. . . . I [didn't] know what I looked like. . . . I remember I was about seven . . . and all my friends [were] Chinese because you couldn't really be anything else. So we were playing and . . . parents could come to the fence but they couldn't come in. . . . I was playing with one of my friends and her mom called her over and said something to her and she came back and said, "I can't play with you because you're black." I was like, "No I'm not! What do you mean? What do you mean?" I was really confused and I was just so sad that she couldn't play with me. . . . I went home and [said to my] mom, "Linda said she couldn't play with me because I'm black!" My mom said, "Well," . . . and I was crying. . . . She put me on the toilet seat . . . and she was wiping my face and . . . she said, "Remember, you're both, you're not just Chinese, you're not just black, you're both." And I was like "But I didn't know I was black." She said, "No, you're not. . . . You're both." And I couldn't get that. . . . I thought you had to be one or the other at the time. . . . When the girl said I was black I didn't understand because I thought . . . we were Chinese because we were surrounded by Chinese. . . . But my mom said, "You're both. You're both." And I said, "Okay,

okay." I was crying, I didn't understand what it meant. [Amanda Wilson]

This was, quite literally, a defining moment for Amanda. Through this first explicit conversation with her mother, Amanda is told that she isn't just one or the other, but both. Amanda's Chinese American mother tried to make sense out of the confusion Amanda experienced by feeling ethnically Chinese, but not looking "racially" Chinese. In this way, Amanda's nonsynchronous experience as an ethnically Chinese American girl with more African features was normalized through the alternative identity framework that her mother provided.

Only in a few cases did students note their parents spontaneously talking about their heritage or identity. For Alex Bell, the family's mixed heritage was discussed overtly, especially by his European American mom:

> [My mom] would just ask me if I was comfortable. And she [say], "I know it's really hard . . . moving and everything. I know that you're getting a lot of static at school, but you just gotta be proud . . . of who you are." I mean, she couldn't offer answers for me, you know? . . . But she would just ask me how I'm doing, am I doing okay? She would be, "Are you upset that me and your father got together? Do you wish sometimes that he married a black woman or I married a white man?" And I would be, you know, "That's not even [possible], I don't even think about that 'cause it's not that way. If it was that way, then it'd be different. But I'm not going to think about something that can't happen." You understand what I'm saying? I'm who I am already. She was probably concerned about me disliking one part of myself. . . . "I don't like being black," or "I don't like being white." I'm sure she was worried about that. [Alex Bell]

Kay Meki's Japanese American father subtly shared his perspective on his daughters' identities:

> I remember my dad telling us [this] story. . . . For awhile he was telling it quite often. Like [a] bedtime story he'd . . . rock me. . . . Or whenever we're eating *ampan* [he'd say] "You girls are just like *ampan*." [It's] sort of a custard roll, [or] sweet bun, and you fill it with *am*, [which is] the red bean. They're sweetened and . . . pureed. . . . And the *pan* is a bread . . . I think for him . . . because it's a Japanese

> sweet . . . (they don't really have *ampan* here) . . . but it's a
> Japanese sweet that was influenced by Western bread-
> making. . . . So maybe that's why he likes that idea the
> best, because it's sort of Americanized Japanese, or West-
> ernized. It's Japanese food, definitely Japanese food, but
> it [is] Westernized. [Kay Meki]

Through his *ampan* metaphor, Kay's father describes his daughters as being Japanese in origin (or at heart), yet having a Western
European influence (in appearance and/or in experience). Sheila
Rafkin's dad also views his children as ethnically and racially diverse. She recalls how "my dad ingrained it into my head, 'Never
forget what other half you are.'" Alluding to her white phenotype
and mainstream cultural experience, Sheila believes her father
would say this to remind her to take pride in her Native American
Indian ancestry while respecting that she was also Irish American.
While these comments are insightful, students who never had such
conversations suspect their parents see them as an extension of
themselves or do not even view them in terms of ethnicity or race.

By contrast, many students remember having conversations about
their mixed ethnoracial status with siblings:

> My sisters, we have the same take on our identities. We
> know where we're coming from, we know things about Japa-
> nese culture. [Kay Meki]

> [I talk about it] more with my middle sister Laura, be-
> cause . . . she's torn a lot by it. . . . She doesn't know [what
> she is]. . . . Recently she's identified more with her Indian
> background. . . . She's more active now, I mean, there's
> always the question of "You're Indian, but you don't look
> [Indian], you still look kind of white." There's always that
> question. [Prakash Moghadam]

> I think the person I've talked about [being biracial] most
> is with my sister. . . . She has felt a lot the same, the way I do.
> But I think . . . she identifies more . . . with being white. . . . I
> don't know, but we have talked about not really totally
> feeling inside one or the other, you know. . . . And my other
> brothers, I haven't really talked to them too much about
> it. [Marta Elizondo]

Students noted how their discussions with siblings yield fruitful
insights into issues they face as people of mixed heritage, includ-

ing concerns about testing by peers from reference groups, questions around their racial ambiguity, and feelings regarding cultural validity, as well as of being both an insider and outsider.

By contrast, Sandy Zubaida feels that talking about being Iranian and white as a child would have been a painful reminder of her difference in a predominantly white school system: "Growing up I didn't really want to [talk about being biracial/ethnic]. I didn't ever want to talk about it I think because when you're in like elementary school or junior high you just want to be like everyone else."

The comments in this section suggest, however, that talking with family members about their unique ethnoracial status can prove to be an important resource for mixed heritage students as they begin to make sense of their ethnoracial heritage.

Physical Dissimilarity

Another theme that emerged from the interviews is how physical dissimilarity among family members affects relationships both within and beyond the interracial/ethnic family unit. Most of the participants share the common experience of having outsiders not recognize their family members as related to one another. Alex Bell explains that being in public with his mom attracts curious stares:

> I noticed . . . that when I'm out with my mom, I *do* get a lot of stares, 'cause she is *very* white. And I do notice . . . that people look at her real funny. . . . Some people that never seen my mom, [and will say] "That's your mom? . . . I never thought your mom was white." [And I'll say] "Yeah, I told you many times I was mixed." What is she going to be? You know? Stuff like that . . . that stuff is funny. That stuff makes me laugh. . . . I mean, it's basically just curiosity. [Alex Bell]

Jocelyn Saghal remembers spending time in Switzerland and how people would react when she was with her Swiss grandmother:

> I'd be walking down the street with my grandmother. . . . I remember hearing . . . from people . . . just because of the way I look . . . my skin color. . . . "This is your kid?" . . . And my dad wasn't there, either, so it was like "Okay. . . . Where's the rest of the story?" [Jocelyn Saghal]

Kay receives varying reactions in public depending on if she's with her Japanese American father, white mother, or light-skinned, blond sister:

> With my dad . . . I think it makes sense because histori-
> cally, one-drop kind of thing. . . . If you're slightly brown or
> mixed then it makes sense when I'm with my dad, then
> they think we're together. . . . Even today . . . I'm with my
> sister and my mom and there was a guy who was sort of
> helping [us to order]. And he wasn't quite sure [if we were
> together]. . . . It's hard. . . . You have to have a public strat-
> egy for dealing. . . . Like, you can anticipate it right away . . .
> and depending on my mood. . . . "Am I going to . . . give the
> cold shoulder? Or make it obvious? Or push . . . their as-
> sumptions back on them?" Right before . . . you can almost
> anticipate it. . . . You're like *"Mom*, what do you want?"
> You definitely say the "mom" thing. [Kay Meki]

Like many mixed heritage students in this study, Kay has come to
realize that her family's range in physical appearance precludes
people from thinking they are related. In order to assuage the confusion and tension this causes, Kay has learned to craft her behavior in public to make the kinship connection clear to outsiders.

Physical dissimilarity seems to impact not only how outsiders
view mixed heritage families, but also how the family members
relate to one another across these differences. For example, Kay
suspects that:

> My mom . . . and my littlest sister Robin have a really
> special relationship. They're probably the closest . . . I think,
> because Robin looks like her. . . . So I think that is influ-
> encing my mom a little bit . . . not in any obnoxious way. . . .
> I guess that's a big deal for mom [to have somebody] that
> looks like her. [Kay Meki]

Although subtle, Kay feels that her mother is affected by having
two daughters who are so physically dissimilar from her, facilitat-
ing a unique bond between her and the more similar daughter.

In a few families, students note how internal or external concerns over the physical dissimilarity of family members led to in-
ferences of adoption. For Amanda, her physical dissimilarity from
her Chinese American mother led strangers to assume she was
adopted: "I don't look like her at all. . . . She's a Chinese woman, I
don't look like her. . . . Everyone used to think I was adopted when
I walked with her. So that bothered me a lot [Amanda Wilson]."

A couple of students describe how siblings played with their physical dissimilarity through tales of adoption aimed at the lightest (in
these cases, whitest) looking sibling. For example, Marta says her

Anglo-looking brother became the subject of an adoption myth among her siblings:

> I don't know how it happened but all . . . four of us, when we came to the new high school, were classified or registered as Hispanic. And then my youngest brother [Greg] when he got registered [he] was registered as white. . . . I don't know how that happened, but we used to always take it out on him. I mean . . . we always use to print that he was adopted and all that and I don't know, maybe it was based on . . . at the time, he was a lot lighter skinned than we were. . . . If you look at the family, my youngest brother is the one that looks most like my mom. . . . The rest of us, we used to always tell my youngest brother he was adopted, and . . . we used to torture him because he looked so much different. [Greg's] not totally different but he was the lightest of all of us and his eyes are almost like my mom's, and his face shape and everything. [Marta Elizondo]

Conversely, Yvonne says she frequently jokes with people about *not* being adopted:

> I think I look like my mom. Exactly, probably. And that's why I always joke that I'm not adopted, 'cause there's no way. You know? 'Cause . . . my sister doesn't look like my mom at all. People don't even believe that they're mother and daughter. [Yvonne Garcia]

These comments suggest that many mixed heritage students learn at an early age how the dissimilarity of skin tone and features within their families challenges people's traditional notions of kinship.

A Unique Experience?

Finally, respondents were asked to talk about their perceptions of interracial/ethnic family life in comparison to their same heritage peers. Do they feel their households are similar or different? The students in this study overwhelmingly believe that their family experiences are different, although they often have a hard time explaining why, as Marta and Amanda illustrate:

> No, but I can't put my finger on why I say no [it's not the same]. I think it was very different for us but I don't know [why]. [Marta Elizondo]

[It's] obviously not the same . . . they can't be the same. . . .
I'm sure there are issues [in common]. . . . But it's different. I can't explain [why], but it's different because I have
different parents. . . . Because it's how . . . parents raise . . .
[kids] . . . their values and stuff. That's totally different—
things are different. [Amanda Wilson]

Still other students suggest that being from a mixed family is more
complicated or difficult precisely because of their interracial/ethnic
character:

No, because it's not the same thing. . . . [As] a person from
a mixed race [background], I not only have to make a
choice . . . [in] the way I talk, walk, act around others,
[and] choose to live my life. But, also, I have to deal with
people around me in public . . . how they see me. . . . And I
think that has to do with people on the outside looking in.
[Donna Tesh]

[It's] different. . . . I know that it's difficult for people who
come from mixed backgrounds. But yet I don't think it should
be outlawed. . . . But I recognize that it's not easy. . . . I
would characterize it as more difficult. . . . Because you all
of a sudden have other things that average, whole-heri-
tage people don't have to deal with. [Yvonne Garcia]

Probably [different]. 'Cause [same heritage students would]
be, like "I'm definitely just checking this one box." You
know? . . . It would be easier. [Melanie Newheim]

Jocelyn explains in detail how she and her cousins think the cultural fabric of her family is less tightly woven than that of her Indian relatives:

No, I don't [think our experiences are similar]. . . . Like my
[Indian] cousins . . . always thought we were so lucky 'cause
we got more freedom because my mother's Swiss. . . . So [to
them] that meant . . . just 'cause their values were different. . . . I got to do more things. And they were getting
arranged marriages. . . . So it was like they admired certain things about my life and I admired certain about their
lives. . . . I always admired and liked the fact that they . . .
are very close. [Jocelyn Saghal]

With the exception of the Karen Loomis, who is third generation mixed heritage, all the students in this study learn to view their heritage, and often their home cultures, as nontraditional because of their multiple nature. Growing up within an interracial/ethnic family structure is seen by these mixed heritage students as different from the norm and characterized by a unique set of challenges as well as benefits that will be explored in future chapters.

SUMMARY

Even if never discussed overtly in the home, these mixed heritage students have a clear sense that their families are unique. For those of first generation descent in particular, the distinct interracial/ethnic status of their families and often intercultural atmosphere within the home leads to a sense of difference that ultimately encourages the development of a mixed heritage frame of reference. While these students' identity orientations vary (as will be discussed in coming chapters), their shared mixed heritage orientation reflects a nontraditional experience in U.S. society.

As recent research attests, effective and high-quality instruction must draw upon students' home and community experiences. In the case of students from recently mixed backgrounds, we must examine our current strategies for addressing the needs of diverse student populations and develop alternative languages for dealing with such nontraditional experiences. We must think about how these students can be affected by data collection processes in registration and testing, counseling practices, curricular representations, school and community relationships, and campus-based social organizations. But first, educators and administrators must consider how mixed heritage students make sense of their ethnic and racial experiences. Toward this goal, in the following chapter I will look closely at how mixed heritage students come to understand and approach their ethnic identities.

NOTE

1. Sandy's story also points to the subjective nature of ethnoracial categories. It seems that from her mother's perspective, the markers of ethnicity and race distinguishing the "Latinos" from the "Persians" were not readily visible to her.

Chapter 4

Lessons of Community: Origins of and Approaches to Ethnic Identity

In a multiethnic society, the notion of ethnicity fluctuates both in its application and relevance in people's day-to-day life. Greater mobility and intergroup contact are shifting the contents of ethnic group life (which were never static) and creating a cultural milieu that is increasingly hybrid. Within such a dynamic context, ethnicity continues to be reinvented generation after generation and yet interpreted in different ways.

In this chapter, proximity and distance (both temporal and spatial) are consistent themes that appear as I explore how mixed heritage students learn about ethnic group membership and consider the nature of students' participation within their heritage groups as children and adolescents. As discussed in Chapter 2, the role ethnic ancestry plays in a person's overall identity formation is described as ethnic identity. While phenotype, the third dimension of ethnic identity, is clearly a mediating factor in the ascription of ethnic group membership and, thus, ethnic identity development, this chapter will look most closely at the cultural dimensions of ethnic identity (history, values, beliefs, and behaviors), including language and dialect. If, as Phinney (1995) contends, some mixed heritage people are at the "interface" between cultures, what can we learn from the discourses these students construct around ethnic identity?

The chapter initially explores what factors influence ethnic identity in the family and beyond. This first section, "Ethnic Identity and Community," considers sociocultural factors at home, includ-ing family stories about community and relatives' experiences with prejudice. Student interactions with relatives and other members of the ethnic group, religious community participation, and the role of language are investigated. The sources of ethnic identity among this group of mixed heritage students are diverse and variably rooted across heritage communities. The cultural medium of the home (as potentially a reflection of both parents' backgrounds) may be influenced by such factors as divorce, remarriage, geographical and generational distance from a heritage community, as well as parental orientations toward ethnic identity and the particular gender/ethnicity arrangement. This last finding suggests that lat-ter-generation women (especially European Americans) often play an important role in preserving the more recent-generation spouse's culture in the home. Ties between the family and broader ethnic community are affected by community demographics as well, spe-cifically access to a heritage community as determined by local popu-lation ratios, and the specific history of intergroup relations between heritage groups. Frequently, one or both parents are geographi-cally distanced from their heritage group, making the family an ethnic island within the local community.

The chapter continues with the section "Student Perceptions of Ethnic Identity" which details student discourses around ethnic identity, which are informed by their parents' identity orientations as well as their own particular experiences within a heritage com-munity. The findings suggest that mixed heritage students tend to embody distinct and flexible identity orientations toward each heri-tage community; these orientations are woven together to present a unified, often fluid whole. If expressed on a grid, such an orienta-tion would be plotted as multiple and shifting points that coexist along two identity axes: one a "postethnic" approach and the other an "applied" approach. Their accounts suggest that an identity ori-entation may express elements of either approach, and that either orientation may shift in dominance over time. This holds true es-pecially among the first generation mixed heritage students who fashion conventional terminology to craft a language suitable for describing their hybrid cultural experiences.

ETHNIC IDENTITY AND COMMUNITY

Patterns of Culture at Home

We learn the meaning of ethnic group membership from our par-ents, extended family, and broader ethnic community. This section will explore how mixed heritage students learn about their ethnic communities through exposure to specific customs, practices, attitudes, and historical knowledge in the home.

When asked to discuss what membership within a particular ethnic group means, many students point to the more noticeable markers of ethnic group life. Specifically, food, music, celebrations, and language are seen as meaningful expressions of ethnic group attachment in students' homes. Melanie Newheim, the only second generation person of mixed heritage in this study, is European American and Mexican American on the side of her maternal grandparents. Melanie says she enjoys participating in certain traditions and practices that reflect her Mexican ancestry:

> I can be ... involved with [my Mexican heritage through] ... my Spanish classes at school. ... Next semester I'll take Spanish II. ... And my grandma ... cooks ... at least two Sundays a month. ... We all get together and have dinner. ... I was supposed to make a Spanish meal [for class and] it was a project that I wanted to do. ... She [knows] a lot of stuff ... [and] during those kind of times ... basically I feel more Hispanic. [Melanie Newheim]

Melanie finds meaning in her Mexican identity when she is actively engaged in things she defines as clearly Mexican, in this case preparing and enjoying Mexican food as well as learning to speak Spanish. For her, being Mexican is more a matter of choice and interest in heritage than of everyday participation since Melanie lives in a mostly mainstream context, although there are strong Mexican American communities nearby. Sheila Rafkin says her mother, who is third generation Irish American, insures that their Irish heritage is celebrated in her family:

> We'd always celebrate St. Patty's day, and ... we usually have a corned-beef-and-cabbage dinner. ... She loves to listen to bagpipe music. She loves to listen to pipers. She has a couple tapes and I made her a tape of some pipers. ... My favorite rock group is Irish. [Sheila Rafkin]

In Sheila's family, food, music, and the holiday celebration are important markers of her Irishness. Like Sheila, most students readily point to these outcroppings of material culture when describing how they learned about their respective ethnic communities. These material dimensions of group life are often the most salient, if not the only landmarks of ethnic identity for many students.

The source and nature of the ideational aspects of ethnic group life tend to be more difficult for many students to articulate. For Sheila, the more ideational dimensions of her Irish identity are introduced largely through resources her parents bring into the home: "Every year we'd watch *The Quiet Man*, the John Wayne movie. And [we'd watch] programs about the Irish. . . . We learned about Ireland. There are a lot of movies about Ireland" [Sheila Rafkin].

Learning about what it means to be Irish is somewhat of a conscious project in her family's household, achieved in part through videos and educational programs about the Irish community. Sheila's father, who is from Minnesota and is Chippewa, brings his ethnic background into the family life in similar ways:

> Occasionally, we'd watch programs [about Native American cultures]. . . . [My dad] has books . . . about the Indians and especially about . . . his tribe. He's from the Chippewa tribe. And he has books about Ojibwa, Chippewa, I think some Sioux . . . children's books written by Paul Gobel . . . they're really good. [Sheila Rafkin]

Like several other students in this study, Sheila learns about the nature of ethnic group identity at home through her parents' conscious integration of their ethnic experiences. The patterns suggest that some parents choose to consciously teach the children about their ethnic identities when they are generationally or geographically distant from their respective ethnic communities. In this way, cultural transmission within the home becomes formalized through a conscious process of enculturation.

Still, for several students, learning about their heritage communities is a more unconscious experience. In Amanda Wilson's family, her parents' Jamaican and Chinese American backgrounds provide the backdrop to everyday life, although to varying degrees:

> There are a couple of Jamaican dishes . . . [dad] cooked . . . every now and then. . . . He told us a lot of stories . . . about him growing up. His culture . . . was not as tangible because there were no holidays, no . . . like real Jamaican holidays . . . there was nothing there that we could see. [And] different things that [my mom] did . . . especially the Chinese New Year celebration. . . . My mom back then [was] really overly superstitious. She still held . . . some of those superstitions . . . like you can't wear white in your hair because that

means death. [I could] never wear [a] white hair . . . bow. She was like "Don't wear that," [and] was really bothered by . . . what I'd wear . . . in my hair. And something about washing your hair on like the first day of something. . . . I never used to understand [why] and I'd be . . . frightened. . . . So some of those little superstitions kind of crept in. [Amanda Wilson]

Growing up close to a large and vital Chinese American community, Amanda's Chinese heritage featured prominently in her daily life.

[My mom's] side was the side I grew up with most, because they were in New York City . . . in Chinatown . . . or New Jersey. And . . . I went to elementary school in Chinatown and so I would see my grandparents a lot of the time, a lot of the cousins and stuff. We'd have the Chinese banquets and New Year's celebrations, all that stuff. [Amanda Wilson]

As a result of her close ties within this community, Amanda can more readily point out the Chinese American influences in her childhood, although she does note that her father's culture was present in the home but to a less obvious degree. Like Amanda, several mixed heritage students feel that one or both parents' cultures were unself-consciously reflected in the home environment.

Of the nine mixed heritage students with one latter-European American parent, most do not recall any signs of ethnic group attachment in the home. These same students, however, easily discern cultural elements in the home which they attributed to the racialized minority parent. Sandy Zubaida illustrates this point when asked to describe what it means to be Persian American, and what it means to be European American:

I never gave much thought . . . to my being Persian except when it's . . . brought up in questions of ethnicity and stuff like that . . . [but] when we'd go to Persian restaurants, or go out with family friends who were Persian, I don't know if I felt differently, but I definitely felt *more* Persian. Otherwise, I don't know. I don't know how much Persian culture was infused into my life. Like, I don't remember anything about Iran just because I was so young when we left. . . . My dad would listen to Persian music . . . watch the Persian channel, and [he] makes Persian food. But day to day living, it was pretty much your basic family in California. [Sandy Zubaida]

The last sentence of the quotation captures how most students with one latter-generation European parent tend to view the parent as not having an ethnic identity or culture. From Sandy's perspective, her Iranian heritage stands out in sharp contrast to the mainstream backdrop of her mother's latter-European American heritage. Among this subset of students, the home culture tends to be described in terms of bas-relief with the heritage of the racialized minority parent providing the cultural detail.

Marta Elizondo, Yvonne Garcia, and Prakash Moghadam are the only three students in the group who describe their home cultures as firmly grounded in one heritage community, which in each case is that of the father. For Prakash and Marta, the home culture reflects the ethnic heritage of the racialized minority parent:

> I'm close to my Indian side because my parents emphasized that a lot when I was a kid. . . . I knew a lot about [Indian culture]. We eat Indian food all the time, my dad listens to Indian music all the time at home. [Prakash Moghadam]

> There's a lot of [Mexican] culture and traditions that we did live. . . . We always had piñatas for our birthdays. We always celebrated the Feast of our Lady Guadalupe, which is a very, very important saint in the Catholic church . . . particularly for Mexicans. And there's a day that's associated with her. . . . Food, that was another big thing. We had a lot of Mexican food. [Marta Elizondo]

Prakash believes his mother, who is third generation Croatian American and German American, consciously chose to stress her husband's heritage even though there are vital local German and Serbian communities in the Chicago area:

> My mom is not really as tied to [her ethnic heritage]. And she also emphasized our Indian background . . . when we were younger. She kind of . . . adopted it too, as a way of showing us that we should adopt it. . . . My mom really made it a point to jump into Indian culture. So when we were younger, my mother would sometimes wear saris and she would do a lot of things at school [related to Indian cultural events]. [Prakash Moghadam]

Like Prakash, Marta emphasizes the role her mother (who is latter-generation German American and second generation Italian American) played in emphasizing her husband's ethnic background:

My mom learned how to cook Mexican food, which is really cool . . . [and she participated in] weddings and stuff. . . . She never questioned it. . . . But my mom is also very much of the line of thinking too . . . [that the] husband is the center . . . or the head of the family. . . . She talks about how she wanted to make the kind of food that he likes so she learned how to make it. And she tells me she goes to Spanish-speaking movies with my dad . . . just because she just wants to be with him . . . she can't understand the film and what's going on, but just [wants] to be there with him. . . . And that must be hard for my dad, to sit in a film . . . and know what's going on and . . . you can't share it with the person next to you. . . . Anyway . . . mom adopted a lot of those things because of my dad, to make my dad feel comfortable and she never questioned it, really, just [to] make it part of our family. [Marta Elizondo]

Although she never learned Spanish, Marta notes that her mother has developed the facility to shift into a Mexican American, or Chicano, dialect:

You know what's funny is . . . I've heard my mom [speak in a Chicano dialect]. And in fact . . . my mom will be talking with my aunts and she'll start [speaking it]. . . . She doesn't know it. I'm like "Oh my God, Mom, you're not Mexican, you're not Chicano and you're picking it up!" [Marta Elizondo]

Growing up within a predominantly Latino context, Yvonne was raised for most of her life by her Japanese American mother:

I would say living in National City [San Diego, CA], it was very much the Mexican experience. . . . The fact that we [frequently] traveled to Mexico . . . hung out more there. . . . I would say growing up we weren't really influenced by [our Japanese American heritage] at all, well . . . very little. [Yvonne Garcia]

Like Marta and Prakash, Yvonne feels her mother did not emphasize her Japanese American background as much as her ex-husband's Mexican heritage (her parents divorced when she was three):

You know, it's weird, 'cause . . . my mom's Japanese, but her parents were born in Hawaii. . . . I guess I know that

I'm Japanese, but . . . [it's] not like her culture was really
strong in my upbringing at all. . . . My mom speaks Spanish [now] too. . . . I think also 'cause she's from Hawaii . . .
it's so diverse there, so mixed. I guess certain things come
into play, like the fact that . . . we have white rice . . . every
day. That's a Japanese thing. . . . But my mom . . . I would
say, transformed into another culture. She really took on
the Mexican culture. She now . . . really likes Mexican
music, really likes to speak Spanish. And her name's Linda,
which is Spanish. Right? And that's just weird because . . .
Linda Garcia . . . really sounds Mexican, you know? [But]
she looks [Japanese] like me . . . a little darker. . . . She
speaks Spanish and she's really taken on a lot of the culture. . . . I would say more so than even her culture that
she grew up with. Because it doesn't seem like my grandparents were . . . strictly Japanese in any sense . . . they
didn't speak Japanese at home or anything. . . . [It's] not
that she didn't have a culture, but it wasn't very specific. . . .
So I think that's probably why she was more open to other
things. [Yvonne Garcia]

Yvonne suspects that her mother's interest and openness to different cultures may be due to her latter-Japanese American heritage,
her exposure to diverse cultures in Hawaii, and the family's proximity to the Mexican American community.

In these three cases, Marta, Yvonne, and Prakash see that their
mothers' decisions to emphasize their fathers' backgrounds helped to
set the monocultural tone of the family. Perhaps available gender
roles encourage these latter generation ethnic women to emphasize
their husbands' more recent, minority heritage. Local population
ratios may play an influential role as well, however only in Yvonne's
case did the community reflect the father's background.[1]

Religion

Religion can be an important component of ethnic group identity. Religion is emphasized to varying degrees in students' families, and only one student feels religion plays an important role in
one of her heritage communities. Generally, participation in a religious community follow three trends: families that do not attend
church at all (n = 5); families that are affiliated with one church
and religion (n = 4); and families that participate in multiple religious communities (n = 6). Most students' families in this study (n = 9)
participate within a religious community, at least when they lived

at home. In four of these families, the students were encouraged to explore religious communities. Three of the four families that encourage their children to try different religions have parents who participate in two distinct spiritual communities, which may suggest that children from such interethnic families are encouraged to be open and tolerant toward religious diversity. Of the six families who did not participate in a religious community, four are headed by the only parents who are divorced and who never remarried.

Among the families that associate with one church, students describe varied experiences within the religious community. Yvonne says her family attended a Catholic church for one year and eventually stopped attending when her parents separated. Melanie Newheim's mom and stepfather are devoutly Catholic, but their church attendance is described as irregular. Missy Connor's family regularly attends the church of Christ Scientist with her mom, stepfather, and brothers. Marta is the only student in the study who says participation in a religious community was consistently emphasized beyond church attendance:

> My parents did everything they could to keep us in the private schools [in Oregon], number one for the education, but also for the religious aspects. . . . They sacrificed a lot to keep us in [Catholic schools]. . . . Religion was a very important part of our upbringing. [Marta Elizondo]

Even though church attendance varied, Melanie, Missy, and Marta suggest that religion was an important aspect of their home life. Yet for Marta (who identifies ethnically as Mexican American) being Mexican American means being Catholic. It is her Catholic heritage, in fact, that brought Marta's parents together at the church function where they first met.

Of the six students who say their families participate in multiple religious communities, Amanda, Donna Tesh, and Sheila say they have attended different churches at various points in their lives. Amanda was brought up in the Lutheran tradition, while Donna attended an Episcopal church with her mother, who was raised Catholic in Panama. Now both Amanda and Donna identify as bornagain Christians, an identity Amanda shares with her mother and brother as well. Sheila says her family used to attend an Episcopal church when she was younger, although she comments on how her mother always supported her when she explored other religions and attended different churches with her peers.

Sandy, Prakash, and Jocelyn Saghal, whose parents come from distinct and strongly religious backgrounds, also were encouraged to explore their spirituality. With a Catholic mother and a Baha'i father who are both active in their religious communities, Sandy says she and her sister were raised to explore and participate in both churches. She recalls how attending Baha'i events with her father put her in touch with the small, local Iranian-American community:

> It's nice. Basically, there are feasts. . . . It was through the Baha'i faith [that] I saw most of my parents' friends who were Persian. . . . It was nice to see them and to talk with them. . . . I'd feel a little out of it because they would talk Farsi. My dad and everyone would go back and forth, then go back and forth, but it was nice, it was good. [Sandy Zubaida]

Sandy also suspects her parents expected her to choose one religion at some point, which she believes she will never do. Prakash says he and his sisters were brought up participating in both his father's Hindu community and his mother's Catholic community.

> My dad's Hindu and my mom's Catholic, [and] they didn't really press either. Neither of them pressed . . . it was kind of . . . my own decision. If either one of them wants me to go to church or temple with them [I] go, out of respect I go with them. . . . My mom . . . she goes ten times a year to church, or something like that. It's not every week. . . . And my dad goes once a month or something like that. It doesn't really have anything to do with a set schedule . . . it's whenever you need to go to temple. [Prakash Moghadam]

Jocelyn's mother was raised Protestant, her father was raised Muslim (now nonpracticing), and they were married in a non-denominational church. Jocelyn explains that even though she was baptized in a Protestant church, her mother still encouraged her to attend churches of varying denominations with her peers.

Unlike Marta, whose sees her ethnic and religious identities as intertwined, Sandy, Prakash, and Jocelyn seem to identify their religious upbringing as something that is a part of their experience, yet more representative of their parents' respective ethnic communities. This may be due to the fact that out of the four students, Marta is the one who identifies most consistently as monoethnic. Also of interest is how in these three cases above, the children were raised to explore the distinct religious traditions of their parents, and sometimes beyond. This was true even for Prakash, whose home environment is more representative of his father's heritage.

The patterns suggest that interfaith families that are open to their children's spiritual exploration may encourage a greater tolerance for religious pluralism.

Also notable is how religion is stressed in only one out of five families with parents who are both latter-generation ethnics. This contrasts sharply with families who have at least one immigrant or recent-generation ethnic parent. In these cases, eight out of the ten families participated regularly within a religious community.[2] Religious participation increases to 100 percent in the four families where both parents are recent ethnics. Finally, divorce may affect the degree to which religion is stressed at home, since four of the six nonchurch attending families were headed by the only divorced parents in the study who have not remarried. These finding suggest that while the nature of religious group participation varies among this group of mixed heritage students, religion generally plays a greater role in the home cultures of families with more recent ties to their ethnic communities.

Language

Language can be an essential dimension of a person's ethnic identity. In this section, mixed heritage students reflect on the nature of language within their families and heritage communities. English is the primary language in the homes of these mixed heritage students. Almost half of the students (n = 7) come from homes where one or two parents natively speak a language other than English; natively speak English and another language; or speak an English patois. Of these seven, only one student was raised bilingually and spent her early years living in a non-English dominant country. These students believe their parents raised them as English speakers because it was the common language within the mixed marriage, and/or because it was in the best interests of the children in light of the international dominance of English, as well as the linguistic chauvinism they themselves faced. Table 4.1 details the seven students' linguistic heritage by parent (this does not include dialect).

Many of these students with bilingual parents note how their family lexicons developed a unique linguistic blend of their parents' home languages. Several say their mothers tried to learn their husbands' first languages, and more than half of these students (n = 4) were trying to learn a heritage language at the time of the study. This latter group of students considers knowing a language to be an important part of cultivating a strong connection with an ethnic community, yet as with religion, few feel their parents expect them to maintain or acquire their home language.

Table 4.1
Foreign Language History of Parents by Student

	Marta	Yvonne	Donna	Sandy	Amanda	Kay	Prakash	Jocelyn
Mother	English	English	Spanish	English	Chinese	English	English	French German
Father	Spanish	Spanish	English	Farsi	Jamaican Patois	Japanese	Malayalam Tamil Others	Punjabi Hindi

Among the students whose parents have diverse linguistic backgrounds, only Sandy was raised in a truly bilingual context:

> When I lived in Iran I spoke . . . Farsi and English. . . . I was fluent in Farsi, I had no problem communicating . . . no problem whatsoever. . . . Then I came [to the United States] . . . [and] my dad never spoke Farsi in the house, really. I know he did in Iran, [but] not here at all. [Sandy Zubaida]

After moving to a predominantly white suburb in the San Francisco Bay Area, Farsi was not emphasized in the home and Sandy quickly lost her fluency in Farsi. In Jocelyn's household, English was the logical choice for her multilingual family:

> [My dad] speaks Punjabi and Hindi, and my mother speaks French, English and German. . . . In India, English is one of the three official languages . . . so he grew up speaking British English. . . . I guess they shared a common language which was English. . . . That's the only language that they shared. . . . So that's why I . . . didn't learn Punjabi, I didn't learn German. [Jocelyn Saghal]

Living in an English-dominant society and having multilingual parents was not the only reason for speaking English in Jocelyn's family. She and Marta both note how their fathers' experiences with linguistic prejudice in the United States was another factor that may have influenced their preference for speaking English at home.

Although English was dominant in the home, these seven students say they were introduced to their parents' heritage languages in different ways. Amanda recalls how her father would playfully "slip into patois and we'd love it. It's very slight now that he's been in the United States for so long, but he can bring it back up." Sandy, Amanda, and Jocelyn say their mothers attempted to teach them Farsi, Cantonese, and German respectively. Amanda's grandparents also taught her some Cantonese words:

> [I knew] my grandparents . . . for a short time before they died . . . for like two years (they didn't talk to my mom after she married my dad). But when they did kind of get reconciled I learned a lot from them [They were] from China . . . [and] they taught me how to write my name in Chinese characters. . . . [They] gave me a Chinese name and helped me write it . . . things like that. [Amanda Wilson]

Although not used regularly, their parents' heritage languages are seen by students as a meaningful part of their parents' ethnic background.

Melanie, Kay, Marta, and Yvonne say they have learned or are trying to learn the language of one of their parents. Marta, Jocelyn, and Yvonne feel that not knowing the language does influence their sense of ethnic identity:

> I started learning Spanish . . . in high school and I chose Spanish because . . . it was a way to identify back to my family. I know that was [a] conscious decision. . . . As the years have gone on, my strong desire to be better and better [in Spanish] has definitely . . . been an attempt to feel more part of the culture. . . . The times that I feel furthest from the community is when I can't understand subtleties of the language—idioms and slang, and things like that. And that makes me feel less and less Mexican when that happens. [Marta Elizondo]

> It's really important for [East Indian] kids to speak their language. . . . It's, like, disgraceful if they don't. . . . [Usually] they will grow up speaking that language first . . . whenever there [are] family functions, whenever they're . . . at home. . . . [Indians are] very tied to their language. . . . So maybe when . . . visiting the Indian conferences . . . maybe if I spoke the language, I wouldn't feel like an outsider. [Jocelyn Saghal]

> Some [of my friends'] parents only spoke Spanish, so that's kind of a big deal. You go over to someone's house, or even

calling someone on the phone . . . and . . . thin[k] "I don't
want to say it wrong." And I know I mess up things. But . . .
the parents are real nice about it. . . . Sometimes they'll try
to speak English. And I think that's really nice, trying to
accommodate me and stuff. So . . . whenever I called one of
my friends and the parents spoke Spanish I got nervous. . . .
[Also] at recess, if [the other kids] were all making jokes
and saying a lot of slang words which I [wasn't] familiar
with in Spanish, I felt different. . . . In general . . . I can
understand . . . 95 percent [of Spanish]. . . . But, yeah,
that's when I started realizing that maybe I'm not as Mexican as everyone else 'cause they all speak Spanish. They're
a lot more . . . Mexican. . . . [And] the fact that I don't look
Mexican [means] people . . . speak Spanish in front of me . . .
[and] thin[k] that I don't understand. That's a very difficult experience because what do you do? Confront them?
Say "Oh, I know what you're saying"? . . . Like, yesterday
in the store. . . . You have these little weirdo guys talking
about you in Spanish, making comments. Me and my sister are sitting there, like, "We know what you're saying."
And it's not funny. . . . I think that's been a big deal to me
because . . . I really am into [the] Mexican side of my culture. . . . I'm really proud of that. But when you have your
own people . . . talking about you in that way, that's kind
of difficult. [Yvonne Garcia]

Here, these students speak poignantly about how a lack of language fluency contributes to their sense of marginalization within
the ethnic group. In addition to not knowing the language natively,
feelings of marginalization can be compounded by physical appearance, as in this case of Yvonne whose more Asian features preclude
her from being seen as someone who is a native speaker of Spanish. Learning a heritage language may provide some mixed heritage students with a means for gaining greater access and legitimacy
within the ethnic group.

Another dimension of language diversity is described by Kay,
Marta, Sandy, and Amanda, who say there is a linguistic syncre-
tism that has developed in their homes. Here, Marta, Sandy, and
Kate Goka explain how Spanish and Farsi are woven into their
family lexicons:

My dad always speaks with his brothers and sisters in
Spanish. . . . I always . . . heard it even though I had not

spoken it myself. And there were certain words that we did know like "*Vámanos*" and "*Andale*" . . . those kinds of things . . . little commands. [And] *chancla*, it's colloquial, but it's the word they would use for those sandals . . . the flip flops. . . . They would spank you with those every once in awhile, "I'm going to go get the *chancla!*" [Marta Elizondo]

I know [words in Farsi] like "Don't touch that!" . . . "Come and eat!" and a few random swear words . . . whatever would come out of their mouths. And [my parents] would use [English and Farsi] interchangeably. . . . Like *mast* is the word for yogurt. And until I was like twelve or thirteen I thought that there were two words in the English language for yogurt—*mast* and yogurt." [Sandy Zubaida]

My dad sort of culturally translated a lot of Japanese things. Like . . . in Japan we have the things called *agi* . . . a dried tofu stack sort of thing—very strange. And you can make *sushi* out of them, *inarisushi*, and they look like a football. So a lot of Japanese Americans call them footballs. . . . We go hang out with our grandparents and say "Ok, you made a football." Or other things [my dad] would tell [my youngest sister], "Robin, eat the chicken bag, eat the chicken bag," [but] he would never call it *agi*. So [my sister] had no idea what the Japanese terms are because he's culturally translated them. [Kate Goka]

Some of the English-speaking parents have learned to negotiate their spouses' heritage language by either picking up some words or even learning it. As mentioned earlier, Yvonne's Japanese American mother learned Spanish. Sandy's mom learned Farsi well enough to teach it formally to the children at one time, but says "[her] Farsi is rusty . . . she can communicate fine but . . . my dad would always make fun of her." Marta explains how her mother manages to interact with her Spanish-speaking in-laws:

She's picked up a few [words in Spanish] a little bit of stuff. And she claims . . . she understand a lot. . . . She talks about how she used to have conversations with my grandmother and my grandfather. They'd speak in Spanish and she speaks in English and they could communicate, which I totally understand. I think that happens all the time. [Marta Elizondo]

In these ways, mixed heritage students are exposed to a range of experiences related to their heritage languages.

The accounts in this section show that even when English is the language of the household, students may be exposed to elements of their parent's heritage language(s) through use of the language with relatives or friends, code switching between the languages, and the integration of non-English words, phrases, or concepts within the family vocabulary. Although they are one generation removed from these heritage languages, the students describe them as significant features of their parents' ethnic backgrounds, as well as the respective ethnic community. There are several possible reasons why none of these students feels pressured by their parents to maintain the minority language. One may be that these parents have adapted to their multilingual marriages by adopting English, thus viewing it as the language of the home and of their children. As well, a language minority parent who has experienced linguistic chauvinism would not wish a similar experience upon his or her children. And finally, language minority parents may be acutely aware that English is a high status language both in the United States and abroad. These latter two explanations will be considered later in the chapter.

Dialect

Dialect can be yet another linguistic feature of ethnic group life. Among this group of mixed heritage students, a small number (n = 4) maintain that a nonstandard dialect plays an important role in their heritage groups. As a result of shifting back and forth between community contexts, these students describe consciously or unconsciously learning the local dialect as a way to adapt to group norms and ensure greater inclusion within the community.

For some students, the acquisition of a nonstandard English dialect is not achieved in the home. Three of the four students say they were introduced to the dialect outside of the home. Marta, who is thirty, says she only recently acquired the ability to code switch between Chicano and standard English:

> I do [code switch]. . . . I hear myself talking to my friends who talk [in a Chicano dialect] . . . and I don't have a problem with it. . . . The only time I feel self-conscious is when my brother's around or when other people [are around] who know I don't normally speak like that because I feel like I'm being fake and I'm not trying to be fake. . . . What I've heard, it . . . is like empathetic listening . . . a way of

unconsciously . . . accommodating the person you're talking to . . . coming to their level—not down or up—but just
being at their level and making them feel more comfortable. . . . So I can do the Chicano English and sometimes I
do it unconsciously . . . I don't do it on purpose. . . . I definitely did not grow up with that. [Marta Elizondo]

Marta underscores that although Chicano English was not spoken
in her home, she has unconsciously picked it up since moving back
to a predominantly Mexican American community near San Francisco as a senior in high school. Marta also emphasizes how this
unconscious shifting between dialects becomes visible to her when
she code switches in front of people who know Chicano English is
not her native dialect.

Moving between two communities provides an opportunity to
learn the differing cultural rules and styles of each context. Further, the relative frequency of this mobility seems to influence the
degree to which learning the juxtaposed cultural norms is more
incidental or intentional. Kris Dawson's ability to speak black English was never very strong when she was in grade school, and it
has decreased over time:

I felt funny talking properly when I was with people who
were talking black [English]. . . . I never could switch it on
and off [and] it became more rare. . . . [I] sort of lost the
talent or something. And I felt fake doing it . . . I didn't do
it right and . . . I just quit. Lately . . . there are subtle little
things that happen when I'm around someone who's . . .
black. I think . . . when I'm around some friends who are
talking very black, then I'll try to [code switch in] subtle
ways. . . . [But] I don't think I really try to talk like that
anymore. . . . I finally stopped doing it. [Kris Dawson]

Speaking black English is more of a conscious project for Kris, although she suspects that she unconsciously shifts to some small degree. On a predominantly white campus, Kris feels the identity politics
within the black community are often too difficult to mediate:

By sort of staying in the white group [I'm] sort of closing
myself off to having relationships with black people. But . . .
when I'm in . . . a group . . . of . . . just black people that act
more black than I do . . . I feel like I'm twelve and I'm at
this middle school party again with all of these black people
and I don't fit in. So I think I've always felt like . . . I would

have to start talking black or somehow I would have to
prove to them that I was cool enough to be a part of that
group. And I just sort of [feel] like it would always take
more effort than just hanging out with the white people.
[Kris Dawson]

Kris's self-consciousness about speaking standard English affects
the degree to which she participates within the black community
at Lakeside University. Donna Tesh began to acquire black English as an undergraduate at this campus, but with similar results:

My roommate tells me I'm terrible at [speaking black En-
glish] because . . . I didn't grow up speaking black ver-
nacular or anything like that. I grew up in a white-bread
type of area, you know. . . . But as far as like every day
speech . . . [I] don't talk black English. I'm pretty much at
home with that realization now. . . . I don't really try [any-
more]. . . . I figure people should take me for what I am.
But there [were] definitely times, mostly during my college years, where . . . I would veer a little bit in that direc-
tion, but not much. . . . I never was in a situation where I
was really trying to be in a black sorority or . . . constantly
trying to fit in. . . . You know, when you see . . . friends who
are just code switching . . . as hard as they can. . . . I never got
to the point where I was . . . trying really hard to fit in. . . .
It was more a thing of when I would see people and . . .
think about what they were thinking about [me] . . . how I
dress or how I act and stuff. [Donna Tesh]

For Donna, tensions around belonging in the African American community were less a matter of linguistics than other cultural factors. Watching others attempt to shift gears between mainstream
white society and the African American community, Donna feels
that her sense of cultural difference cannot be overcome by consciously adopting the local norms of behavior.

Of the four students who find dialect to be important to a heritage community, Alex Bell is the one who grew up speaking a nonstandard dialect in the home. For Alex, "acting black" and speaking
black English are essential dimensions of his ethnic identity. Living in both black and white community contexts, Alex has encoun-
tered a great deal of intolerance toward his black dialect:

I'm more comfortable talking black English. And sometimes
people . . . think it's a sign of respect if I talk to them in

standard English. And I will be, "You know that's funny because I'm talking to you in black English because I do respect you—you know? . . . It means I'm comfortable around you." And that's hard for people to understand. When I tell them that, they're like "Whoa! I didn't know." My Japanese teacher, I've known him for years . . . I was pretty comfortable with him, so I [spoke] black English and he's all, "How dare you speak to me like that. Use proper grammar." And I was, like, "Excuse me?" [And] th[is] girl . . . her mother's always correcting my grammar. It used to make me real angry because people I'm comfortable around, or certain surroundings I'm in, I'm going to talk a certain way. I'm going to talk black English. [Alex Bell]

Alex has spoken with his mother and thought deeply about this issue. Earlier in his life, Alex felt pressured to adopt standard English in order to survive in a predominantly white community. After moving back to his current, more diverse neighborhood, Alex now is inclined to challenge people's intolerance and defend the appropriateness and legitimacy of black English:

My mom brought it up [and said] . . . if I had . . . an accent or something . . . and [my teacher] didn't like my accent . . . would [he] ask me to change? . . . How can you ask somebody to do that? . . . If all I've ever talked is black English, how you going to ask me to talk standard all of a sudden? . . . [My teacher said] "Well, it's not the same thing." And I'm like "But it is . . . you're closed-minded. . . . And that's not on me, 'cause as long as you can understand me, I don't see why there's a problem . . . that is a real dialect, sir. It's real." And he's all . . . "Oh, I never thought of it like that . . . I'm just trying to do it for you 'cause you're not going to get a job talking like that." And I'm, like, "You're probably right." But . . . if I really have to talk proper English to get a job, I can switch. . . . That's what I told this girl's mother. . . . "You know it's funny because . . . I was comfortable around you, that's why I [spoke] that [way]. But you made me uncomfortable by . . . always correcting my grammar." And she's all "Oh, I didn't realize that." [Alex Bell]

Still, Alex does code switch when he deems the occasion calls for it:

When I meet new people, I switch. I'll talk standard English. That's about it. . . . People that can't understand me,

sometimes they be, "What are you saying?" And I be, "Oh,
my bad." So I'll switch. I'll be, "Okay, you understand now?"
[And they'll be], "Oh, that's what you're saying." [Alex Bell]

Through these experiences, Alex has learned that his home dialect
and preferred cultural style is seen as disrespectful, even substan-
dard and in need of correction, within the white community. While
code-switching is a way to meet the cultural demands of the context and avoid marginalization among all four students, clearly the
toll of marginalization is far more costly for Alex whose way of interacting with the world is stigmatized by mainstream white society.

The findings in this section detail how dialect is an important
feature of ethnic group membership in some communities. Regardless of whether acquisition is incidental or intentional, becoming
bidialectal entails a certain degree of self-consciousness on the part
of the speaker. Although acquiring the dialect later in life may be
accomplished unconsciously by virtue of spending time in the community, some note how this acquisition is not without tension for
mixed heritage students. Not knowing the local dialect carries the
risk of being seen as a foreigner, or less legitimate, especially within
a minority community. In these instances, acquisition can become
a more stressful process for students. Yet the acquisition of the
mainstream dialect may pose very different types of risks. For Alex,
black English is a fundamental part of his black ethnic identity,
while standard English has been used too often as a yardstick for
demeaning his experiences as a black English speaker.

Community Narratives

Information about ethnic group identity is also transmitted
through the stories relatives share about the family's heritage or
experiences. Most students (n = 10) recall one or both parents overtly
talking about their ethnic backgrounds, although the nature of these
narratives vary greatly.

Among the ten students, a majority describe hearing stories about
distant ancestors through which they learn about their relatives'
lives, and especially about their migration to the United States.
These stories seem to be selected by students because they map out
the family's connection to what they see as a culturally authentic
ethnic community that is both geographically and generationally
distant from their lives. For many of the latter-generation European American students, such stories are the key sources of information about their ethnic ancestry, as Marta describes:

My mom just made references to her grandmother and . . . things that she used to do. She very much loved her grandmother. . . . In fact I'm named after both [her] and . . . my dad's oldest sister. . . . My mom talks about her grandmother having brought a lot of the food and traditions, Italian traditions. . . . But I don't know how to do anything Italian. . . . Once she passed away, then she didn't have that anymore. Like . . . they used to get ravioli for their birthdays . . . but once she was gone they didn't have that anymore. . . . I know they used Italian to some extent, but I don't know how much. [Marta Elizondo]

Marta's idea of what it means to be Italian is based in large part on the stories about her great-grandmother, and her comments convey a sense of loss at the passing of her great-grandmother and her Italian cultural heritage. Talking about European ethnic ancestry as something lost that must be unearthed is another way geographical and generational distance from the heritage community is conveyed. Sandy explains how her "mom was always going to research [her ethnic ancestry] and make this huge family tree. She never did." In these ways, mixed heritage students learn that ethnic group membership among latter generation European Americans is located in the past, beyond their immediate experiences and resurrected through those of their immigrant relatives.

By contrast, students whose parents are immigrants, more recent generation ethnics, or racialized minorities in the United States can recall their parents or relatives sharing stories about their own lives. Amanda and Prakash say their parents spoke frequently about their experiences:

My mom would tell me a lot of stories about when she was growing up in Chinatown, different things that she did. . . . But it was evident and I knew [that] she was [of Chinese descent]. . . . [My father] told us a lot of stories . . . about him growing up. . . . Saturdays were story [days]. . . . His culture . . . was not as tangible because there were no holidays, no . . . like real Jamaican holidays and, you know, there was nothing there that we could see. [Amanda Wilson]

My dad [talked about his ethnic heritage] a lot. We were really tied into my father's background. We still are. . . . [My parents] emphasized a lot about our Indian heritage. [Prakash Moghadam]

In addition to her mother's stories, Amanda notes how material aspects of her mother's ancestry further helped to shape her ideas about what it means to be Chinese American. Sandy gathered some insights into her father's ethnic identity from the infrequent stories about his childhood:

> My dad didn't really talk about his family. He'd talk about his parents a little bit and his sister, but not, I don't think I ever heard him talk about his grandparents. When I wouldn't study, he would tell me how he *always* studied, and I would tell him, "There's nothing else to do in Iran, Dad." Which I know is stupid. But like that's all he would tell me about Iran. So I just figured everyone always studied. But no, he never really talked about it much. [Sandy Zubaida]

These students learn that ethnic group membership is something that directly shapes their parents identities, thereby conveying a sense of proximity to the heritage community that is not afforded the prior group of students.

Community narratives may also speak to the oppressive conditions which inform a group's collective identity. A number of students say their parents have discussed the prejudice they, or other members of the heritage community, have faced. Both Jocelyn and Marta talk about how their fathers' experiences with linguistic prejudice and racism influence them:

> I don't want to place blame [on my father for not teaching us Punjabi and Hindi]. . . . I hate it when people say, "Oh, god, that's so sad. You could have learned so many languages, and that's really unfortunate." That really pisses me off. . . . [They] don't know . . . all the racism that goes on . . . the linguistic . . . [and] the racial stuff that goes along with being a linguistic minority. . . . Especially my father coming [from India] . . . after the first immigration after '65. . . . The first wave of immigrants that were able to come again after all the exclusion acts. . . . People don't know. . . . We're in a different place now. We're in the '90s . . . there's a big difference. . . . It's painful, but I understand why [he didn't teach us Punjabi and Hindi] . . . why he felt like he only wanted me to speak English—'cause he didn't want me to go through things that he's gone through. [Jocelyn Saghal]

> I think it was [my dad's] choice, not to teach us Spanish. . . . I was asking him [about] those things. . . . He used to tell us

about some of the things that he went through. . . . He
used to get in trouble for speaking Spanish in school. . . .
But a lot of the things that he did not perceive as racist . . .
were very much so. I mean, if you looked at it from another
perspective, you'd think "God, you went through this?" And
to him that was his way of life. . . . He kind of accepted
some of that because "That's the way it was." . . . It's so
hard to talk to parents and grandparents about those things
because I don't see them the same way. . . . The choices
that . . . they had to make. . . . My father giving up Spanish, I don't think he's ever seen it the way I did, as a loss. . . .
I think he's very happy and proud that I speak Spanish.
now. But I don't know if he feels the same way . . . [that] he
should have never had to have given it up. . . . I see it as a
giving up and I don't know if he would [see it that way] . . .
[as] a survival thing. [Marta Elizondo]

Jocelyn and Marta realize that the absence of their fathers' primary languages at home is due, in part, to the choices they had to
make as ethnoracial and linguistic minorities in the United States.
Beyond the United States, a few students learned about their parents' experiences with oppression in their home countries:

My dad was . . . the Vice Chancellor of a university [in
Iran], so he was in a close position to the Shah . . . he worked
for him. . . . So I think that has a lot to do with the fact that
he doesn't want to go back. And plus, my Dad's Baha'i, and
they're persecuted over there. [Sandy Zubaida]

My father['s] . . . family literally had to leave when he was
five [with] what they could carry on their backs. . . . It was
India, but now it's Pakistan, where he was born in a small
village. . . . The Muslims were . . . killing [Hindus], literally. . . . I think one of his uncles was killed . . . and cousins
were killed because they were Hindu. So, his feeling about
religion is that it's divisive, it's bad. . . . I grew up with him
really saying, "I don't believe in God, but religion does."
[Jocelyn Saghal]

These narratives reveal the salience of ethnic identity in their fathers' lives by showing students how language, religion, and
ethnoracial status can be stigmatized in certain contexts.
   While community narratives helped to create a sense of proximity or distance to a group, these themes also emerged among stu-

dents whose parents did not discuss their ethnic heritage. For example, Marta and Yvonne suspect their fathers did not talk overtly about their ethnic backgrounds because their family or community experience reflected these backgrounds:

> In terms of my dad's side of the family, we're living [the culture]. . . . I mean, it wasn't like something that was talked about, it was there. [Marta Elizondo]

> I guess I know that I'm Japanese. But really, not like [my mom's] culture was really strong in my upbringing at all. . . . My dad . . . I don't think he ever spoke about it. But the fact that we traveled to Mexico . . . hung out more there. . . . I would say living [South of San Diego], it was very much the Mexican experience. [Yvonne Garcia]

These students' experiences within a Mexican American dominant family or community creates a sense of immediacy, making it unnecessary for their parents to explicitly discuss what it is like to be Mexican American. Conversely, some students suggest that the lack of discussion about their ethnic heritage stems from their generational and geographical distance from the community:

> My mother is Croatian and German. She was born in the United States. . . . Her grandparents each came from Croatia and Germany. . . . My mom [doesn't talk about it], not as much [as my dad] because she's more removed from what her supposed ethnic background is. . . . Some of her extended family is in Croatia still, I never really hear about her German relatives—I don't even know who they are. [Prakash Moghadam]

While an absence of community narratives was common among parents who are latter-generation European American, it was also the case for parents who are distanced from a racialized minority ethnic community through generations of intermarriage within the European American community. This was the case for Melanie Newheim (second-generation Mexican American) and Karen Loomis (third-generation Native American), and Karen's comments elaborate:

> The only time that [my Native American heritage has] really been brought up was like old stories from when we went back to Oklahoma. And I don't even remember, I was like five or six. . . . I've started to ask my parents and we've

tried to find out things, but . . . people who knew so much about it have passed away. It's really hard to get information because my grandma . . . it's either selective hearing or she just can't hear. . . . It doesn't . . . come up in a conversation. . . . That's why I wish my grandfather was still alive, because he was very knowledgeable about his heritage and being Native American. [Karen Loomis]

Unlike the other parents from racialized ethnic minority backgrounds, Yvonne's mother does not construct any community narratives:

My mom's Japanese, but her parents were born in Hawaii, too. She's only . . . second generation. . . . I guess certain [cultural aspects] come into play, like the fact that . . . we have white rice . . . every day [at home]. That's a Japanese thing. . . . But my mom . . . herself . . . transformed into another culture. She really took on the Mexican culture. . . . And her name's Linda, which is Spanish. . . . And so . . . Linda Garcia . . . really sounds Mexican. . . . She's really taken on a lot of the [Mexican] culture . . . more so than even her culture that she grew up with. Because it doesn't seem like my grandparents were . . . strictly Japanese in any sense. . . . They don't have a . . . formal religion. They didn't speak Japanese at home or anything, and so I don't [speak it]. . . . I think also 'cause she's from Hawaii and it's so diverse there, so mixed. . . . I think that's probably why she was more open to other things. But . . . growing up we weren't really influenced by [Japanese culture] at all. Well . . . very little. [Yvonne Garcia]

Yvonne suggests that her mother's cultural upbringing in Hawaii and distance from a traditional Japanese American community may contribute to her openness in adopting the local Mexican American culture. Local population ratios and, as mentioned earlier in this chapter, gender may also be factors that influenced Linda Garcia to support her ex-husband's culture in the home.

Clearly, narratives of community are not the only means through which a sense of ethnic identity is cultivated. But these accounts suggest that stories are significant sources of information about the nature and meaning of ethnic group membership for children. Although they embody differing approaches to ethnic identity, these narratives may sustain ethnic affiliation in the home when there is distance between the individual and heritage community due to generation, geography, or interethnic marriage.

Community Ties

Beyond the home, student participation within the broader ethnic community, specifically through relationships with relatives and peers, provides important cues about the nature of ethnic identity within the group. For students with European American ancestry, ethnic identity among relatives and peers is not seen as particularly salient. Karen exemplifies this perspective as she talks about her friends:

> I don't really pay attention [to ethnicity]. . . . I guess . . . all my friends who I hang out with . . . look white. And I noticed in . . . my English class . . . there were a lot of Hispanic people and a lot of white-looking people and . . . only one African American person. . . . I don't pay attention. Although . . . when I took P.E. I noticed there are very few white people in the class. . . and then the rest were like a lot of Hispanic people. . . . But I don't really notice [ethnicity]. I really don't pay attention. It's important, but . . . not important [that] I have to know. [Karen Loomis]

Asserting that it's not important for her to know her friends' ethnic backgrounds, Karen clearly notices race. In this way, Karen is like most of the latter-generation European American students in this study who are more likely to see themselves and others in terms of racial identity rather than any one ethnic identity. Even though all of these students have lived in predominantly European American communities, ethnicity is not considered an important dimension within these contexts.

By contrast, ethnic identity is seen as much more salient when students describe their participation within racialized ethnic minority backgrounds. For some students, visits with relatives provide the only opportunities outside of the home to discuss their ethnic-minority heritage. Opportunities to interact with relatives and peers varied greatly, however, depending on local population ratios and other factors which affect access to a particular heritage community. Often participation within a community was infrequent, as Sheila notes:

> A long time ago we used to go to the pow-wow. . . . We haven't been able to go lately . . . partly because of finances and also partly because we haven't [received the] dates [for it]. . . . I remember going for a day . . . and . . . all the

good fry-bread. That was the one thing I loved. And at the fair one time, they had a stand-up comic who was a Native American and he told jokes. There was also a stand where they sold buffalo burgers. . . . So those were good experiences. [Sheila Rafkin]

Outside of the home, Sheila's connection with other self-identified Chippewa or Native Americans were limited by the population ratios of her local community. In addition to the more material, pan-Native aspects of her heritage she details, Sheila describes elsewhere the importance of the relationship she developed with her paternal grandmother, who lived with the family for more than a year when she was four. Most of the students also say they are geographically distanced from relatives on one or both sides of the family due to immigration. Of the seven students with foreign born parents, Amanda, Kay, Jocelyn, Prakash, Donna, and Yvonne have all visited or lived in one or both of their parents' home countries. Sandy is the one exception:

My dad's never been back [to Iran]. I'd like to go back, [but] my dad says it's not safe. I have a grandma and an aunt over there. . . . They leave [them] alone because they're two old women [and] they're not going to . . . start anything. . . . [But] my dad [says] going back to Iran . . . would be very dangerous. [Sandy Zubaida]

A small number of mixed heritage students had access to a sizable minority-heritage community, as Prakash describes:

We would go to a lot of Indian functions in Chicago when we were young. . . . My dad is really active in [the] Indian Medical Association in Chicago, and there's an umbrella group called the Association of American Physicians from India. . . . Then there's also some Kerala groups—he's from Kerala, which is a state in India. And we would go to . . . a festival called Onam, which is the harvest festival in Kerala. . . . They would always have this big function at our high school and we would go and eat. . . . We're really tight. A lot of our friends are Indian and that's who we hang out with . . . and it's not exclusive. . . . Basically [it is] the circle that . . . my mom and dad hang out with. . . . Just whatever doctors he works with. . . . [And] dance and stuff . . . was a pretty major part of my life when I was a little kid.

Traipsing around with . . . [my sister] Laura . . . who did
the [South Indian] dance. [Prakash Moghadam]

The extensive connections that his family has within the local East
Indian community provided ample opportunities for Prakash to
learn about his Indian heritage.

In these ways, local population ratios often determine the degree
to which students can build relationships within ethnic-minority-
heritage communities. For many students like Sheila, the meaning
and nature of ethnic identity generally are fostered at home. Only
a few students, like Prakash, had access to a robust, tight-knit ethnic minority community. Amanda and Yvonne, the two students of
dual minority heritage, are the only two students who grew up or
participated regularly within thriving majority minority communities for their entire lives. As detailed earlier in this chapter, having peers, neighbors, and friends of the family who were Chinese
American and Mexican American, respectively, had a lasting impact on Amanda and Yvonne.

Distance and proximity reemerge in this section as important
themes affecting ethnic identity development. Beyond the home,
both the nature and relative frequency of students' interactions
within their heritage communities are varied. Among students of
latter-generation European American heritage, ties with other
multiethnic European Americans is common and reinforces the
optional approach to ethnic identity that is learned in the home.
By contrast, ties within the ethnic minority community are not assured for mixed heritage students and the home may provide the
only source about the nature of identity within the group. When
local population ratios or travel to a heritage country allow, the
ensuing relationships within the minority community allow mixed
heritage students to learn more about the group and the experiences of its members. The next section will explore carefully the
affects of such different experiences on students' approaches to ethnic identity.

STUDENT PERCEPTIONS
OF ETHNIC IDENTITY

The prior section attempts to illuminate how ethnic identity is
shaped by experiences in the home and broader ethnic community.
The section that follows explores how mixed heritage students perceive their ethnic group membership in light of such experiences.
Their comments reveal that students embrace multiple orientations

toward ethnic identity, each aligning with a particular heritage community and often shifting over time. Students' identity orientations can be loosely plotted as multiple and shifting points along two identity axes: one a "postethnic" approach and the other an "applied" approach. Hollinger's (1995) work is helpful to describe one axis as a "postethnic" orientation, or an approach toward ethnic identity that lacks any salience in daily life beyond the objective fact of one's ancestry. A postethnic orientation is best characterized as situational; like a hat, it is something that is reached for voluntarily and donned on certain occasions, but does not correspond in any meaningful way to a person's day-to-day interactions. Among mixed heritage students, this orientation is seen mostly in relation to their latter European American heritage. Students are more likely to use a national label or racial label (e.g., "American" or "white") than an ethnic descriptor to describe their (usually multiethnic) European heritage. However, this approach also is seen in relation to minority ethnic heritage among the two latter-generation mixed heritage students who are more generationally distant from these communities.

The other axis represents a more lived, or applied approach toward ethnic identity. In this orientation, ethnic identity is seen as emerging out of one's daily experiences and interactions in the world. From an applied orientation, ethnic identity is an essential, inseparable part of daily life and cannot be taken on or off like a hat. This approach is most evident among a few students in relation to their minority ethnic heritage.

Perhaps indicative of their diverse and dynamic experiences, ethnic identity among these mixed heritage students is reflected in a myriad of orientations which cannot be easily summarized as a single, overarching approach. The following section picks up on themes presented earlier and details how students come to see the meaning of ethnic group membership as mediated by community approaches to ethnic identity, participation in cultural traditions or practices, and the acquisition of language, dialect, cultural knowledge, and behavior.

Transparent Ethnicities

When asked to describe what it means to be a member of a particular ethnic community, many students were unable to do so in terms of their latter generation European ethnic heritage. Among these students, the cultural markers of an ethnic group life are not readily detectable. Melanie Newheim explains "It doesn't mean

nothing to me, I don't know why. 'Cause I haven't learned about
what it [means] being Caucasian or white, you know?" Melanie's
comments underscore how the dominance of European Americans
in U.S. society, and their absence within popular multiculturalist
discourses, render them invisible in cultural terms.

For those students from majority–minority backgrounds, the cultural contours of European American life are implied when they
describe the contrast that exists between their heritage communities. By making a comparison between groups, mixed heritage students delineate what their European ethnic heritage is *not*, but not
exactly what it is culturally, as Alex and Marta demonstrate:

> See, it's something that we all don't want to admit. But it's
> a fact that white people act a certain way and black people
> act a certain way. Of course, you can draw . . . certain in-
> stances out when it's not that way. But on a whole level it
> is that way. On a social level it is that way. [Alex Bell]

> I don't know what Italian and German is. . . . We didn't
> grow up the way [my Italian and German relatives] grew
> up. I mean, my mom had a lot of farm experience and that
> was . . . American. . . . My German family has a farm. . . .
> We . . . visited the farm and . . . participated in a couple of
> family events, but that felt like a family thing. We do this
> family reunion every year. . . . But I don't know if that's [a]
> cultural thing. Fishing was something they always did, and
> I don't know if that's a cultural thing. I mean, I don't asso-
> ciate . . . the[se] things [with culture] . . . [like I do] on the
> Mexican side . . . foods, and language, and customs and things
> like that. . . . The kinds of things we do on the [German–
> Italian American] side don't sound like . . . [the] same cat-
> egories. . . . The fishing and camping. . . . I don't know if
> those are culturally based. [Marta Elizondo]

Both students speak to a cultural dimension of European American life, although Alex does not expound on its cultural contents
and Marta is not fully convinced it is cultural. While most students
can't find the words to describe what it "feels like" to be ethnically
European American, their remarks reveal that it is much easier to
identify racially, as Donna's statement illustrates: "I don't know if
I feel white . . . I don't know. . . . I don't think of myself as white. . . . [It]
has a negative connotation for me . . . [which is] neither here nor
there. Just, I wouldn't want to be identified as white [Donna Tesh]."

When asked to consider her European American ethnic identity on its own terms, Donna can only describe it in terms of race.

Many of these mixed heritage students suspect that there is a cultural dimension to their experiences as latter-generation European Americans, but they do not have a frame for interpreting their lives in a cultural way. The ethnocultural elements of mainstream culture are multiethnic in origin (yet highly influenced by Anglo-Saxon Protestant traditions), and their predominance in U.S. society make them seem transparent among latter-generation European Americans. Thus, most of these students tend to approach their European American identities from a postethnic orientation, seeing themselves as less marked by culture and more bound by race.

Primary Connections

For a few mixed heritage students, the meaning of ethnic group membership is found through their relationships with family members and relatives. As discussed earlier in this chapter, generational distance and local population ratios constrain the degree to which students can build relationships within the heritage community, especially minority communities. This may influence why some students identify so strongly with particular family members when describing the significance of their ethnic identity. Melanie, for example, is second generation Mexican American and has lived in a diverse but predominantly white community for her entire life. Although there is a strong Mexican American community close by, Melanie contends "[Being Mexican American] has meaning to me because of my grandpa." Kris speaks in a similar way about her European American heritage, and explains, "Being white, for me, means a connection with my mom's side of the family." Amanda was raised with strong ties to a vital Chinese American community. Although she visited Jamaica twice yearly with her family, Amanda still looks to her father when discussing her Jamaican identity:

> [Being Jamaican] means being my father's daughter. I think that's all because I'm not sure even what Jamaican culture is. . . . The food wasn't that big a deal, it's a small part. But I think of who my father is . . . that's what I see as Jamaican culture. [Amanda Wilson]

Jocelyn has lived in India for six months and has visited Switzerland. She says "One of the things [being Indian] means is . . . that I

really know my father. . . . It makes me feel really [a part] of my
grandmother. . . . So [being Indian and Swiss] has to do with . . .
relationships . . . on both sides." And finally, Kay sees her sense of
ethnic identity as influenced by the specific statuses of her parents:

> I think that [being European American] . . . has more of . . .
> a gender politics because of my mom. . . . In college I read
> a lot of Cherríe Moraga and she has a lot of stuff about
> [how] your ethnicity is gender, especially if you're mixed,
> you learn race and ethnicity through gender. . . . I was
> doing women's studies and ethnic studies and it was like
> [representative of] both my parents, in a way. I was out
> there fighting for a woman, for my mom, and I was fight-
> ing for my dad. I mean, obviously it's more complex than
> that. . . . I think my understanding of who I am as Euro-
> pean American is very gendered, and it's through my mom's
> type of experience.

Kay elegantly details how the respective identities of the parents
can play an important role in how one learns to be an ethnic, racial, and gendered person, especially within an interracial-inter-
ethnic family.

The important role family members play in students' sense of
ethnic identity may have more to do with growing up in an interethnic family structure than either geographic or generational distance alone. A parent or relative is often a child's primary role model
of, and connection to, a heritage community. In this way, a family
member may come to symbolize the heritage community and all of
the experiences or relationships a mixed heritage child has within
that community. This does not mean, however, that students themselves do not feel a part of the ethnic group. In fact, the students
mentioned adopt a wide array of approaches toward their ethnic
identities that reflect their diverse experiences within their heritage communities.

Material and Ideational Dimensions
of Ethnic Identity

The material aspects of a community's culture are most frequently
presented when mixed heritage students describe the meaning of
their ethnic group membership. Several students refer to specific
cultural elements that shape their sense of ethnic identity, such as
food, customs, traditions, celebrations, and holidays enjoyed with

their parents, friends, and families. Prakash and Marta are two of these students:

> I identify as Indian . . . like I cook Indian food. . . . I listen to Indian music and I'll read Indian history sometimes. [Prakash Moghadam]

> My particular interest in the kinds of foods I eat and the kinds of music I listen to, and some of my hobbies and the festivals I go to and the way I celebrate things and the way my family celebrates things . . . that's all Mexican American. . . . Also . . . there's a very particular saint's holiday that is celebrated by all Mexicans and we celebrated it very devoutly every single year. . . . [It] still actually holds a lot of value for me. . . . I enjoy that particular tradition and that's very specifically Mexican. [Marta Elizondo]

Such outcroppings are easily identified by students as symbolizing a particular group's lifeways.

Students note how they adopt certain attitudes and behaviors which are representative of their ethnic identity, emphasizing both material and ideational aspects of culture:

> I think it's facing the holiday things again . . . that was a big deal. And just the respect for elders and stuff. . . . With my grandparents, we always had to say to them "Good morning" in Chinese, and not say certain things around them. . . . I remember there was a lot of respect there and . . . the importance of family [is] part of it. [Amanda Wilson]

> Just recently . . . me and my girlfriend broke up, and I found myself really emotional. . . and you don't usually see brothers do that, you know? To be honest with you, we're hard, you know? We ain't crying or nothin' like that. And . . . I found myself crying. . . . I sort of . . . wrongly classified that as acting white . . . but I know all people can do that. . . . It's just, black people on the whole, they see that as a sign of weakness, so they don't do it. But white people are, like, "Oh, it's okay, cry. Let it out." [Alex Bell]

> Being Irish? It explains some . . . things. Like why my mother behaves [the way she does]. . . . And the Native American explains why my father behaves [the way he

does]. . . . It explains some of the traits I have. [Sheila Rafkin]

Some students say they have inherited their parents' culturally-inspired outlook toward life, or worldview. Sheila says her beliefs about the ecology are derived from her father:

> There's a . . . closer contact with nature (in Native American Indian communities). . . . Some of the things [Indians] do to stay close to the nature. . . . When people start talking about the environment and . . . when I watch things about nature and about the troubles going on with endangered animals. . . . I don't know if it would sound general or not, but Native Americans have always been a little more closely-knit to [the] ecology. . . . My Native American side usually kicks in when I think about nature and about the environment. [Sheila Rafkin]

Even though her mother's German and Italian relatives are Catholic, Marta believes that her religious identity is tied more to her experiences as a Mexican American:

> Being Catholic . . . the religion . . . that's a very, very deep seated part of how I grew up . . . that whole perspective. . . . You can take different views of Catholicism itself, and I think that whole take as very mixed in with [being] Mexican American. [Marta Elizondo]

Kris makes evident the relationship between her European American heritage and her sense of identity: "I think [being European American] makes me feel a little more connected with . . . history and just society as a whole. I feel more like I fit in." Because she was raised by her European American mother in predominantly white communities, Kris's comments detail how her worldview reflects a mainstream orientation.

The Politics of Ethnic Identity

The political nature of ethnic identity also informs students' sense of community membership. Like other students in the study, Yvonne talks about how her ethnic experience is shaped by her family's socioeconomic status and her father's immigrant background:

Mexicans and Chicanos do have an experience . . . especially . . . a low income [experience]. . . . Back in school everyone's kind of . . . the same income. Everyone's not really . . . rich, no one's really poor. But we're all . . . kind of in the same struggle. When you go [to Lakeside University], it [is] a lot different. You star[t] seeing these big differences. Even within the Chicano community, you have upper-class Chicanos, too. . . . And that was something new for me. . . . I realize that . . . what I identified with the most were Chicanos and that [low income] experience. [And] my father was from Mexico. . . . I related more to that than [to] Asians. [Yvonne Garcia]

Sheila and Jocelyn explain how power, privilege, and oppression inform their heritage communities:

As for being oppressed, I understand that . . . history and how other races might feel [because of my Indian heritage]. . . . With Irish, too, I understand about being oppressed. . . . I learned about how much the Irish were persecuted, especially in America. And I find it interesting that both halves of my race are from persecuted types of people. [Sheila Rafkin]

[Being Swiss], it means that I have access to privilege. Like, I can get my Swiss citizenship. [Jocelyn Saghal]

A few students bring out their experiences with prejudice and racism as having a deep effect on their sense of ethnic identity. For Alex, these experiences mostly occurred while living in a predominantly white community:

It was hard [living in the suburbs]. . . . My mom would be "What's wrong?" And I'd be "Things that they said at school." The teachers couldn't believe I was so intelligent. And the kids . . . they didn't want to pick me [to play with them] for nothing. . . . They'd be "You're not part of us, you're not one of our kind." And I knew all white people weren't like that, 'cause I had my mother and everything. So it was real confusing for me—how somebody could act like that—'cause it was the first time I'd ever confronted that. You know, you read about it or whatever. You hear about it. But until you really confront it, you don't know what it is. [Alex Bell]

Kay realizes that her Japanese heritage makes her the target of anti-Asian sentiment:

> Just random people, and not even people I know [would say intolerant things]. . . . Like [I'll be] talking in the store and someone's just yelling at you [because I have Japanese heritage]. That happened a couple of times. So . . . I didn't ever feel like I had a chance, an option, to pass [as white]. I felt like whether I was half . . . [it] didn't matter. The part that meant the most . . . and made me a target sometimes, was the Japanese [part]. [Kay Meki]

As these comments reveal, some mixed heritage students start to develop a political awareness about the import of their ethnic and racial heritage in the U.S. context. This political framework also seems cultivated by the interracial/ethnic structure of their families, as students observe the differences and similarities in experience across their inherited ethnic groups.

Streams of Ethnic Identity

Finally, many students describe ethnic identity as open-ended. This sentiment was strong for the majority of students, who feel it is important to learn more about one or both sides of their ethnic heritage. For some students, visiting their parents' native countries or learning the group's history, language, or dialect (discussed earlier in this chapter) is something they have done or plan to do in the future in order to establish deeper ties with a heritage community:

> I've recently become interested in the Croatian side [of my heritage]. I was to go to Croatia with my aunt in April and I was really disappointed that I couldn't go. I think I'm going to go pretty soon. Because I'm really curious about it. [Prakash Moghadam]

> I don't feel like I fully felt like I was Indian until I went to India and . . . explored that and really asked myself a lot of questions. . . . [Being Indian] means . . . being from a culture that's really rich in history and experience. [Jocelyn Saghal]

I think I see [being black Panamanian and Dutch American] as a cool thing. . . . The fact that I can . . . explore several components of my own . . . identity . . . makes me excited to bring that . . . hopefully [to] my children. [Donna Tesh]

Yet, learning more about her Japanese heritage for Kay magnified the cultural differences between her experience and those of her Japanese relatives, "Japan . . . it's a totally different consciousness and tradition and culture. . . . I was kind of shocked because that's the real thing."

This desire to learn more about one's ethnic group seems to stem from a tension students feel between their ethnic experiences and the traditional criteria of ethnic group membership. The fact that a person has ancestry linking her to a particular ethnic community does not guarantee she will feel like a full, card-carrying member of the group, especially if she is of recently mixed heritage. Learning the history, language, dialect, behaviors, beliefs, and practices of a group are ways mixed heritage students deepen their connections with a heritage community. Fourteen of the fifteen students in this study feel their sense of ethnic identity will continue to unfold in the future, revealing the open-ended nature of ethnic life among this group of mixed heritage students.[3]

SUMMARY

The chapter attempts to unpack the numerous factors that influence how mixed heritage students make sense of ethnic identity. Among the first-generation students in particular, the roots of ethnic identity are complex. Because of their recently mixed heritage, students tend to see themselves as ethnically dissimilar from their parents, who are viewed as representatives of their respective ethnic communities. Especially among those with foreign-born parents, being East Indian and Swiss means something vastly different for the person who is both a second-generation U.S. citizen and of dual ethnic heritage. The cultural experiences of mixed heritage students are not mirror images of their parents' lives. There are striking differences in terms of culture (usually bicultural or diasporic), language (English dominant, standard English dialect), phenotype (often representative of "looking mixed"), and, I would add, socioethnic status (multiple heritage), the primary elements of ethnic identity. For these reasons, discourses of ethnic identity among mixed heritage students reveal flexible and nontraditional identity orientations. The emphasis placed on one heritage may be greater, less, or equal to the emphasis placed on the second heritage, although the stress placed on either may shift over the course of the individual's life.

Some of the gender patterns discussed invite further research into the relationship between parental gender roles and expectations, ethnic and racial identity, parenting styles, and family culture. Another topic for future investigation may be the influence of material status on ethnic-identity development. Finally, since the group of students featured in this study come from such diverse backgrounds, the themes explored in this chapter may also be examined for patterns by region, gender, and interethnic mix (e.g., European–African American students, etc.). In the next chapter, I will discuss students' lessons and interpretations of race.

NOTES

1. Marta, however, lived in a predominantly Latino neighborhood until the age of seven.

2. This number rises to nine out of ten if Yvonne Garcia is included. The year her parents were married and living together, Yvonne recalls attending a Catholic church regularly.

3. The one student who does not foresee any change to his sense of ethnic identity is Steve Billings, who was a freshman in high school at the time of this interview.

Chapter 5

Constructing Race

In Chapter 4 I examined the types of discourses that students construct around ethnic identity and the roots of these constructions. This chapter looks closely at race, in particular how race is learned through students' relationships beyond the home through their interactions with peers. Individuals acquire knowledge about the norms of group behavior, as well as the nature of a group's racial identity, in large part through social interaction. These interactions also teach the mixed heritage person how their mixed background impacts their group membership, if at all. As a result, mixed heritage students develop the skills necessary for successfully navigating within and across their heritage communities.

As discussed earlier, race is not scientific fact or a figment of the imagination that can be wished away. Instead, race is accomplished and comes to have meaning through people's everyday interactions. Similar to noticing a person's sex, we learn to distinguish certain features as racial, as if they provide information about who a person is in relation to us (Omi and Winant 1993). This process of associating physical and other characteristics with broader racial group membership is learned over time, transmitted both within and beyond the home. Thus, race is done, in part, as people interpret certain features as markers of the individual's relative position in a racialized social structure. Race also is done when the racially ambiguous person is asked to clarify their status within a racial ecology through such questions as "What are you?"

Yet the sociocultural elements of ethnic group membership are implicit in our understandings of race, as well. Many of the mixed heritage students in this study learn (implicitly or intentionally) to present an appropriate "racial" self across different social contexts, especially within racialized minority groups. Altering one's behavior to meet the cultural standards of a social context is one way students can consciously attempt to be less culturally suspect, while for others it is an unconscious response grounded in their experiences within a community. This chapter explores the types of racial work that mixed heritage students engage in, how this work reflects a borderland experience (especially for first generation students), and how it results in a nontraditional, hybrid approach to racial identity.

BORDER BUILDING

One of the ways mixed heritage students learn about race is when their racial heritage is suddenly called into question or made evident to their peers. As a result, borders are assembled in relation to the student to establish their status as an outsider. Amanda Wilson, who is Jamaican American and Chinese American, recalls an incident that occurred while attending a predominantly Chinese American elementary school:

> I went to the bathroom and I was washing my hands. . . . Then [this other student] said in Chinese, "she's black." I understood them, right? . . . I was crushed. I was [thinking] . . . if they said, "You're both" then that would be okay because my mom said that was okay to be both, but not to say one. So when they said "she's black" it bothered me so much. . . . I was like, I know [I'm black], but I'm both [Chinese] and [black]. . . . It wasn't till after elementary that I realized . . . I didn't look Chinese . . . [I was] thinking . . . I [looked] like everybody else. [Amanda Wilson]

Speaking in Chinese, the student emphasized Amanda's black heritage, thereby defining her as racially and culturally distinct from the other girls—as not Chinese. Through this and other interactions, Amanda learned that her physical dissimilarity from her Chinese American peers often precludes her from being seen as a community member, despite her cultural experience and heritage. This incident was one of several which taught Amanda that being "both" Chinese American and Jamaican American did not mean she would readily be accepted as a full member of either community. Amanda was raised to view herself as both Jamaican and Chinese American, and her broader ethnic community of reference at that time was Chinese American. Amanda explains that the bathroom incident disturbed her because in a context where she thought she was Chinese American like her peers, her black heritage was singled out to the exclusion of her Asian heritage.

Yvonne Garcia, who is Japanese American and Mexican American, remembers how her peers also defined her as an outsider at school due to her physical appearance:

> I had just come from Hawaii where everyone's real mixed . . . and there's a lot of different ethnicities. And I went to school [in South San Diego] where there's . . . 90 percent Mexican [students] and very few anything else. And the Asians that were there were Filipino. And so I remember feeling real different. . . . "Oh, they're calling me *Chinita*," and all that stuff. And I was, like, "I'm not Chinese" . . . getting real offended by that . . . [and wondering] "Why are they making fun of me 'cause I look different?" And I guess when I was younger . . . I looked a lot more Asian, and so . . . that's when I felt different. . . . It was . . . other little kids and stuff. Now I look back and it wasn't a big deal, but at that time I remember feeling *real* different—everyone's dark, everyone's Mexican, everyone speaks Spanish, and I didn't speak Spanish.

Yvonne's Latino peers drew clear boundaries, marking her as an outsider especially in terms of her physical difference. In response, Yvonne drew her own lines and appropriately disidentified as Chinese. And like Amanda, Yvonne was not seen as a community member even though she was identified ethnically with this community.

Sandy Zubaida, whose mother is European American and whose father is Persian, describes a somewhat different experience while attending predominantly white schools. After moving to the United States at the age of four, Sandy spent most of her life surrounded by European American peers and identifies strongly with mainstream culture. Phenotypically blending in with her white friends, Sandy now recognizes how borders of difference were constructed around her Persianness, usually in response to inquiries about her surname and place of birth while at school:

> I think most [people] just see me as American . . . I don't look like I'm Persian very much . . . I never gave much

thought as to my being Persian except when it's being
brought up in questions of ethnicity and stuff like that . . .
it's something that stands out and so I guess in that way I
feel different. Growing up . . . I didn't ever want to talk
about [my heritage] I think because when you're in . . .
elementary school or junior high you just want to be like
everyone else. . . . [My Persian heritage would] make me
stand out and be different. . . . So . . . when people would go
around the room and say where they were born, I dreaded
that. I hated it. And so I never really talked about it. I
didn't really know anything about [my Persian heritage]. . . .
It just made me different and I think that bothered me.

Revealing the tacit assumption that Americanness is equated with
whiteness, Sandy describes how the emphasis on her less familiar
Persian heritage made her feel out of place and foreign as a child. She
later explains how this emphasis conspired with her status as the
youngest in her cohort to create a heightened sense of difference.

Border-building interactions define a student as racially (and
culturally) "other," revealing the relational/hierarchical "face of
race." While such differentiation occurs in all communities, it is
especially restrictive in the white mainstream. Phenotypically nonwhite students are viewed as ethnically and racially different regardless of their cultural experiences or racial heritage.[1] Within
the mainstream, rigid standards of whiteness are maintained as
the law of hypodescent is operationalized through such boundary
constructions.[2] The application of the one-drop rule is uneven at
best, however, since many mixed heritage students in this study do
blend into the mainstream, which suggests that the rule is less
guided by genotype in contemporary racial life (at least in this region of the United States).

These examples of border building help to illustrate how many
students in the study find themselves marked as outsiders to a
group because of their racial heritage and/or physical appearance.
It is not the fact of mixed ancestry that relegates a person to non-
member status, but rather one's perceived status as a member of
distinct racial group. Traditional racial logic is mobilized as people
reach for commonly held notions of race and kinship in order to
create order in the world around them. Incidents of border building are, therefore, important sites where mixed heritage students
learn about the nature of the racial ecology and develop strategies
for future interactions.

CLAIMING

Most students shared stories about "claiming" group member-ship which, unlike boundaries drawn to one's exclusion, lead to one's inclusion within a community. Claiming can be initiated by peers or by students themselves and always makes reference to a student's racial heritage as a credential for membership. Prakash describes how looking more European American prevents his recognition as East Indian and encourages him to claim this affiliation:

> Indians will, a lot of times, recognize that I'm Indian here in the United States. But in India, it's not as clear because I'm a lot lighter and because I have European features (I'm a lot lighter in India than most people). . . .. My sisters have more Indian features and I don't, my nose is not Indian. . . . So sometimes [Indians] look at me and automatically know I'm Indian and sometimes they look at me and they think of me as American. . . . It's a way of identifying. I mean, if they're Indian and I'm Indian then that's a bond. . . . If somebody who's Indian asked me [what I was] I would say Indian be-cause that's, a lot of times, what they're looking for. They're trying to determine if I'm Indian. [Prakash Moghadam]

For Prakash, claiming his Indian heritage helps to resolve his ra-cial ambiguity, especially when in response to an inquiry by his Indian peers. Sandy describes an experience at a university in south-ern California:

> There was an announcement in the newspaper [for] a Per-sian club meeting . . . so I decided I'd go. . . . I went and this guy was looking at me the whole time like "You're in the wrong room!" I had to leave early . . . and he said, "Wait! What's your name?" I told him and he was like "Are you half? What are you?" He wasn't mean at all . . . I think he was full (Persian). [Sandy Zubaida]

In both examples, Prakash and Sandy explain how their physical ambiguity can render them unrecognizable within their minority heritage communities. Questions about heritage provide the cul-tural evidence needed to claim Prakash and Sandy as group mem-bers, bridging the gap that exists between how Prakash and Sandy look and how outsiders presume community members should look.

When initiated by mixed heritage students, claiming membership helps to ease this dissonance, but sometimes it may create
new tensions. Below, Amanda talks about a time with her classmates when she claimed her Chinese identity:

> In elementary school we were . . . on a school trip . . . to the
> museum of natural history. . . . There was . . . another
> class passing our class [which] was basically Chinese and
> me, right? And this class of all black students passed and
> they said "Ching chong, ching chong!" . . . I got so mad
> because I knew I was Chinese . . . I turned around and
> said . . . "How dare you say that, I'm Chinese, too! Whether
> you think so or not, I am." And they were like, "You're
> crazy!" And I'm like, "No, I'm Chinese, too." It was a con-
> text . . . [where] I had to defend them because I'm part of
> the black students . . . and yet I'm part of the [Chinese
> students too]. [Amanda Wilson]

As Amanda explains, claiming herself as Chinese in front of the
other students was a subversive and risky act. By this time in her
life, Amanda realized that people didn't see her as Chinese American, and claiming so could lead to painful teasing by either group
of peers. Also, defending her Chinese heritage might have been
perceived by her African American peers as choosing sides and denying her black heritage. Clearly, Amanda felt in the middle; her
choice to affiliate as Chinese "too" placed her in the position of a
bridge between communities as she stood up for her Asian peers
and challenged some of her black peers on their intolerance.

Clearly, the act of claiming is important to a person whose physical appearance belies their identity and/or heritage. Like Amanda,
Missy Connor's appearance is often misleading:

> [Before my friends] got to know me they were . . . like "Oh,
> you're just a white girl." But now . . . since we became re-
> ally good friends, they [say] "You're half Indian." . . . [It's
> like] my friend who I grew up with . . . this girl Maria. . . .
> This boy I was talking to said "Oh, you're nothing but a
> white girl," [to Maria], and we said "Wait a second, she's
> not white." So they kind of . . . jumped at each other. But
> I'm all. . . . "She's not white."

Drawing from Maria's experience as well as her own, Missy explains how her peers are quick to assume she is "just a white girl."

Missy actively claims her Native American Indian identity in order to be recognized as a "person of color" among whites and people of color alike. Kay Meki talks about a time when she claimed her Irish heritage at school:

> I had a class and we were studying . . . Irish American history. . . . [The class] was about different ethnic histories and the teacher was like "Look at the immigration. There are so many people of Irish descent." And she's like, "Everybody raise your hand, who's Irish!" I'm actually Irish and I raised my hand . . . everyone is sort of looking at me. . . . So I think that that's the one time I remember where I did it just for shock value. . . . I'm probably just as much Irish as a lot of those other people who are of German backgrounds [and are] Irish somewhere. . . . It's the same thing for me [but] its sort of shocking for [them].

In these examples, both Missy and Kay choose to claim parts of their ancestry as a way to challenge their peers' assumptions about their racial heritage or identity and redraw the boundaries of group membership to their inclusion. For Kay, claiming was a subversive act because she used it to defy the authority of the one-drop rule. And as Kay notes, the shock value of claiming membership in any community can challenge people's common sense notions about race, kinship, and identity.

LIFE IN THE MARGINS

Most of the mixed heritage students in this study (those of first-generation backgrounds) speak about the subtle and sometimes overt ways their legitimacy and loyalty to a group is challenged by their peers, resulting in their marginalization within the group. These challenges are carried out in various ways and occur most frequently within racialized minority groups. For some students, it's difficult to find the words that best describe just how their sense of legitimacy is contested. Here, Marta Elizondo talks about an ineffable form of exclusion by her Latina peers within the graduate program at Lakeside University:

> Well, there's a . . . definite Latina faction . . . and I very much want to identify with them. And I normally do identify with the Latina culture. But this group has pushed me somehow on the outside and part of it, I'm feeling, is

my mix[ed heritage]. . . . Sometimes I have the feeling that
I don't have the full experience of being full Latina. . . . It's
only certain individuals but . . . I'm starting to feel like
"Ok, where do I really belong, then, if I don't belong with
them?" . . . I feel much further from the white community
than . . . from the Latina community. So I fe[el] way in the
middle.

Despite her cultural experiences and strong identification as Latina,
Marta suspects being mixed makes her culturally suspect within
this group. Her language beautifully illustrates the process of
marginalization from either group's center that placing her "way
in the middle" in the borderlands between white and Latino. Jocelyn,
also a graduate student at Lakeside University, depicts a similar
undercurrent within an Indian American group:

Last year I went to a South Asian [group] in San Francisco, and I'd never been to one. I'd been hearing about
this group . . . and I thought "What better place could there
be for me?" You know to . . . see myself, and to . . . find
people that are like me in some way. But I really didn't
feel welcome in that group at all. It's very subtle . . . very
insidious that [message], "Well, you're not pure Indian. You
haven't lived there for a long time." I've lived [in India for]
six months. . . . That's really problematic for me . . . [to]
feel like [they're thinking] . . . "Both parents have to be
Indian," or "You can't really claim this, 'cause you're not
really Indian." [It was] . . . just very subtle things about
people not recognizing me and myself not feeling comfortable, that [maybe I'm] not pure enough . . . not completely
Indian. . . . It was all very subtle . . . more insidious kinds
of things. . . . Not being welcome in their conversation . . .
body language and . . . just sort of innuendoes . . . that kind
of thing. [Jocelyn Saghal]

Jocelyn and Marta speak to a common tension experienced by many
of the students in this study who describe feeling ostracized by their
peers and relegated to a more liminal status within the group.
Jocelyn has thought deeply about how other Indians may see her
and why she thinks she is marginalized:

I think [other Indians] . . . might say, "Oh, she thinks she's
too good for us." They might say, "Well, we don't really
think that she's going to fit in." They might be thinking

[that] I'm really not that interested in [the Indian] part of me or something 'cause I'm not consistently [a] part of their group. . . . It would be interesting to ask them and have people articulate it. . . . It might be . . . that it is so subtle . . . they don't even recognize that they might be doing those kinds of things. . . . When I was [a teaching assistant] . . . we did that whole multiracial [identity] week and [issues of cultural legitimacy] came up a lot. It also came up in our graduate seminar [when monoracial] students would say "We had people who would [attend our group] and were half-Korean, and half . . . something else. . . . There was always talk . . . behind their backs like, 'Oh, [she's not] . . . full Korean. Like, Why is she here? . . . And . . . people would talk about it.'" [Jocelyn Saghal]

Through these opportunities, Jocelyn learned why mixed heritage individuals may be seen as less authentic, or culturally suspect, because of their mixed status.

As a result of being marginalized, some mixed heritage students develop a sensitivity to these tensions when they interact with group members. Although Donna strongly identifies as African American, she is concerned nonetheless about how her boyfriend's Trinidadian parents will view her as a potential daughter-in-law:

Another weird thing is . . . I know my boyfriend's parents would rather he married a black person for sure. . . . They think I'm fine, [but] sometimes I wonder if I'm black enough. . . . Not that we're going to get married or anything like that, but it's crossed my mind like "How black do they want?" [Donna Tesh]

Similarly, Alex Bell talks about being aware of his mixed status when spending time in a predominantly African American community:

All my relatives back East are all black. I went back there [recently] and it was kind of different for me. I felt kind of awkward because back East is totally different . . . I mean . . . I wasn't sure . . . how they would portray me. Because they obviously could tell [I'm half white]. . . . I *knew* my relatives knew, you know? And also, I didn't know them. . . . So that caused nervousness. I was just really concerned with how they would portray me because . . . they were all black, basically . . . I wasn't really worried, I was just . . . curious as to how they would see me. . . . I mean, granted, sometimes

when I'm around . . . black people I feel nervous, and sometimes when I'm around white people, I feel nervous. And that's
probably because of me being mixed, you know? And sometimes I get confused . . . "How should I act?" And so forth.

Alex's comments show an awareness of how different cultural contexts can have different behavior standards which, if not mastered,
can lead to marginalization by the group.

    Several students say they adjust to the contexts of their heritage
communities and display appropriate cultural credentials by either pushing out certain aspects of their identity, or by actively
blending into the scenery. In this way, mixed heritage students
can try to gain greater legitimacy among their peers and diminish
the risk of marginalization that their mixed status threatens.
Amanda recalls learning too late that her loyalty was being tested:

> [I usually] say, "My dad's Jamaican, my mom's Chinese," or
> vice versa. Either way. I remember once, [with] one person, I
> had said "I'm Chinese-Jamaican." And they said, "Oh, so you
> don't think you're black? You put Chinese first!" And I'm like
> "Does it really matter?" . . . Those people were sensitive. So I
> would just end up saying my father first maybe because I
> look like him—you know, to be sensitive to that . . . de-
> pending on who I was talking to. [Amanda Wilson]

Here, Amanda's response to the "What are you?" question was seen
as disloyal to her black heritage. So her loyalty will not be in question, Amanda now consciously adjusts her behavior by pushing her
black heritage to the fore when other African Americans ask about
her background. For Alex, altering his behavior to match the cultural standards of the setting means sliding back and forth between
what he views as "acting white" and "acting black":

> I was slipping for a while, when I was up there [in a white
> suburb]. . . . I was acting white, 'cause I had to, you know?
> Or I would get ridiculed. But when I came down here [to
> Excelsior], things changed. . . . I was, like, you know,
> "[Black]'s how I want to be." I mean, most of the time I see
> myself acting more black, if you can classify being black as
> acting a certain way. [Alex Bell]

Alex describes how he has adapted to different contexts by blending in and becoming bidialectal. But for Alex, "acting white" means

not being true to himself and his preferred style of interaction. As discussed in Chapter 4, several students say they code-switch with varying degrees of success (although, except for Alex, always to a nonstandard English dialect) as a way to blend in with their peers.

Another way students actively try to blend into the cultural context is by changing their appearance or mannerisms. Here, Amanda talks about changing her mannerisms and hair styles so she doesn't stand out in the African American community:

> Ever since high school . . . I realized that [how I look] was a problem [in the black community]. I made sure to never . . . do anything to my hair . . . [I'd] pull it back into a bun or just not touch it cause it shows vanity or something. . . . People get upset when you touch it. . . . A couple times on the track team . . . (because the track meets were basically big fashion shows) . . . I remember . . . the length of my hair was always an issue. . . . When I first had to run a track meet I would leave my hair . . . in a ponytail and people would be like, "Oh, she thinks she's white!" . . . It used to upset me so bad . . . I have no white in me . . . I'm black and Asian. But they don't know . . . and next would be, "She has a weave." A lot of this happened on the subway . . . more hair things. . . . Just [negative] looks, and the same comments again, "She thinks she's white and she things she's smart" . . . because I was wearing glasses and had a book. Every time . . . the black girls came [they] would hover . . . like purposely around me. . . . I remember . . . one time this guy and girl . . . [were] on the subway. . . . I wasn't doing anything, just standing and breathing. . . . And the boyfriend was apparently looking at me a lot. And the girl said, "Oh, and you think you're so beautiful, don't you?" . . . I wasn't doing anything. . . . And . . . she was like, "Oh she thinks she's so beautiful with her long hair and light skin." And I was just like, "My God!" And her boyfriend didn't say anything. . . . She didn't get mad at him [when] he's the one who's looking at me. She got mad at me! . . . Immediately when I got to college, I wore my hair in a bun every day because I didn't . . . feel like starting . . . off on the wrong foot with anybody. So it was in a bun every day. . . . Yeah, the subway incidents. . . . And also the light skinned thing . . . always added to the hair . . . [what a] wonderful combination. . . . I remember I would always bury my head in a book [on the subway], always. [Amanda Wilson]

Amanda has learned that her features, specifically her skin tone and hair texture, can create tension with other African American women. Amanda, who defines herself as a born-again Christian, recently had an opportunity to discuss some of these tensions with a good friend who is black:

> I have a friend now and we're . . . also . . . close sisters in the Lord because we're both saved. She is very, very dark skinned and she has short hair. . . . I went to Chicago for a wedding two weekends ago and she was there. . . . We were both at the hotel fixing our hair [and] getting ready for the wedding. . . . I was doing my thing, she was doing her thing with the curling iron. . . . She just looked at me, smiling . . . and she said, "You know what? God's really changed me, because in the past I would be hating you right now." And I said "Really? . . . But you're not like that." And she's like, "Well, yes I was. You're the kind of friend I would have hated. . . . I had a friend I hated because of her hair. . . . Every time we walked outside together guys would look at her first and then me, as if I was . . . not attractive." And [my friend is] beautiful, she's so beautiful, you know? And then she kind of joked and . . . said "Well, I guess I don't mind you because you don't flip your hair." . . . She said . . . her ex-friend used to flip her hair all the time and it infuriated her 'cause . . . when they're out [in public] . . . her glory was her hair. . . . I remember ever since high school . . . I made sure never to touch [my hair] or move it or flaunt it or play with it. [Amanda Wilson]

Amanda has learned to play down the physical markers of her "Chineseness," even altering her hair style, mannerisms, and eye contact while in public, in order to avoid negative interactions in the black community.

Still, many mixed heritage students speak about resisting the need to prove their cultural validity by changing their behavior. Jocelyn talks about how she's learned to cope with her marginalization in the East Indian community:

> I stopped going to [Indian events for awhile] . . . [I thought] "I don't have to find my community there . . . I have . . . my other friends." . . . It does make me a little sad because of their reaction, and . . . their values . . . their judgments. But . . . I don't want to put myself in that position, 'cause I don't like feeling that way. . . . So sometimes I don't go . . .

I guess [that there is a] conflict for me. . . . I mean, I still go, but I just don't do everything with them. Or . . . I'm not going to volunteer on their newsletter, or whatever . . . I see them and I know them, but . . . they're not my best friends or anything. [Jocelyn Saghal]

Jocelyn doesn't feel fully accepted in the Indian-American community, so instead of subjecting herself to frequent marginalization, she attends only on occasion and finds her central source of support among her other friends. Alex Bell explains why he doesn't try to blend in with some of his black peers at school, even though this leads them to question his cultural legitimacy:

I don't really have a lot of friends. I tend to have acquaintances—people that I know here and there, people that I be cool with, you know? But I find it hard, to be honest with you, to have a lot of black friends because . . . [the] males at least . . . you know, they're all about doing ignorance. . . . They're all smoking weed and drinking and want to go party all the time. . . . And that's just not me. I mean, it's kind of sad, but I can't . . . interact with that, you know? 'cause they're always wanting to push me and . . . be, "You ain't a real nigger, you don't smoke weed." And I'll be, "You right, I'm not a nigger, I'm glad you noticed that. . . . It's too bad that you are, sir." And a lot of [black] people [say] "You can't be black, you don't smoke weed. He ain't down." I be up, he right. I'm not going to take myself down, right? Yeah, I can't interact with [that]. . . . A lot of my friends that used to be my friends aren't . . . anymore because . . . they do those things now. . . . I remember back in junior high, people didn't do those kinds of things . . . I get a lot of flack in school for being so confident. It'll be, "You're so arrogant, so conceited." And I'll be, "Well, if you had to go through what I had to go through, you'd build up defenses to get through life, too."

Alex observes how more and more of his African American male peers have become involved with alcohol and drugs in high school. Although Alex is careful to point out in other parts of the interview that not all of the black guys he knows do drugs, he does feel that there is a growing pressure to do them and that his identity has been called into question for refusing to participate. Like Jocelyn, Alex describes developing friendships selectively when he can within and beyond the community.

This section attempts to illuminate how being mixed can impact a person's relative status within the group, especially within racialized minority communities. The students' stories detail how looking, acting, or sounding different from their single-heritage peers often leads to a marginalized status. Through subtle and explicit behavior, single-heritage peers establish themselves at the cultural center and relegate the mixed heritage person to the group's margins. This process contributes to a heightened sense of self-consciousness for many mixed heritage students when they participate in their heritage communities.

Mixed heritage students frequently learn to negotiate their behavior to meet the cultural norms of the setting, sometimes in an attempt to combat being assigned to a liminal, or second-class status in the community. By providing "proof" of their cultural loyalty or legitimacy, full citizenship within the group may be attained. Still other mixed heritage students refuse to prove themselves to their peers; these students develop alternate strategies and avenues for participating within their heritage communities without jeopardizing the integrity of their diverse identities.

RESOLVING THE "CRISIS" OF RACIAL AMBIGUITY: FACING THE "WHAT ARE YOU?" QUESTION

Mixed heritage students learn the rules of the racial ecology, and their relative location within it, through encounters with the "What are you?" question. This question is asked of the person with an ambiguous racial appearance and/or name. The following section explores student responses to this question and what lessons they learned about race and mixed race as a result of such interactions.

Among the first-generation mixed heritage students, twelve of the thirteen say they are accustomed to hearing people ask "What are you?"[3] Several students recall being asked this question all of their lives. While Yvonne feels she is seen as more racially ambiguous as an adult, Kay has the opposite experience: "I think when I was growing up (in the Bay Area), when I was littler, it was not the same story. It was like, "What are you? Are you Hawaiian?" or "Are you a Chicana or Mexican?" or they weren't quite sure [Kay Meki]." Also from the San Francisco Bay Area, Missy says people aren't used to meeting people like her who are naturally dark-eyed blondes:

> Well I think [people ask me] basically because they don't think they see blondes with brown eyes. . . . So they've come up to me [and asked] "Where did you get brown eyes, did you put contacts in? Did you dye your hair?" . . . I'd go

"Well I'm half Indian," and they'd go, "Oh, well where are
you from?" . . . I'll get strange questions . . . it's kind of
weird. . . . When I was born I had brown eyes, and [my
parents were told] . . . "They'll change to blue because usually blondes have blue eyes." . . . It didn't seem right . . .
somebody with blonde hair and brown eyes. [Missy Connor]

By responding that she is half Indian, Missy runs into people's assumptions that she must not be a local but from somewhere else.
Eye color can be an issue for people who meet Marta, as well, in
conjunction with her name:

I get asked all the time . . . [but] a lot more . . . in the
Latino community more than anywhere else. . . . A lot of
people will say [my eyes are] green, they change. . . . It
mostly happens where I'm with a group of people . . . it's
either [my eyes] or it's the [Spanish] language . . . I don't
get pegged as being from the United States. But [I'm also]
not [seen as being] from wherever they're from. . . . People
who approach me on the street . . . if they see my name
then I'm [seen as] Latina, right away. . . . And when I walk
into like a Mexican restaurant, it can go both ways . . . who
will address you in Spanish and who will address you in
English. And most of the time I get addressed in English . . .
probably because I'm fair skinned and because of the way
I dress and stuff, too, I'm not typical[ly] Mexican, Latina,
whatever. [Marta Elizondo]

Marta notes how the "What are you?" question in the Latino community stems from people's interest in national origin, but also realizes she is not always seen as Latina.
    Clearly, people attempt to read physical features as if they pro-
vide a diagram mapping a person's racial heritage. Prakash, Kay,
and Donna are aware of this dynamic:

[People ask me what I am] all the time . . . because they
look at me . . . and they don't know. . . . [In the United
States], people ask me everything from "Are you Iranian?
Are you Greek? Are you Italian?" [Prakash Moghadam]

Now . . . there are more and more people who are Asian
and white [in the Bay Area], so people seem to . . . feel they
have a radar or something [and ask me if I'm Asian and
white]. [Kay Meki]

[People will ask] "Are you mixed?" [Like the] teenage girls
[I work with say] "Are you mixed or Mulatto?" . . . People
try to be, like, super [politically correct]. . . . Black is fine.
You can go with mixed. You can go with black. I think because [of my] eyes. . . . Having blue eyes, people get confused but . . . I think it's the kind of question that people
know the answer to before they ask. But they might as
well ask "Are you black and white?" [Donna Tesh]

A number of students say these interactions occur at school:

I remember . . . I was in elementary school, and a new girl
came. . . . She asked me where I was from . . . I think she
thought I was from another country or it was her way of
asking what is your ethnic [background], or something. . . . I
said I don't understand . . . and she said "What nationality
are you?" I said I'm American. But since then, I've run into
that a lot . . . [people] assume I'm not just black and white.
[Kris Dawson]

Alex, who is asked the question regularly, recalls how speaking in
Spanish affected his peers at school:

Yeah, people ask me a lot of times. . . . I was messing around
one day [at school] and I was talking Spanish . . . I have a
good accent. You know? And they're all, "Are you Puerto
Rican?" And I was, like, "No. I'm just messin' with you."
[Alex Bell]

His comments suggest that Alex is aware of his racial ambiguity
and realizes that speaking Spanish will further complicate his racial ambiguity in the eyes of his peers. As a result of being asked
the "What are you?" question repeatedly, mixed heritage individuals learn that elements of their physical appearance are seen by
others as unusual or nontraditional within the racial ecology.

Assuming that others are trying to delineate their heritage or
specific mix by asking the question, some mixed heritage students
have learned to adjust their responses to the question:

I always say that I'm half Japanese and half Mexican. . . .
People . . . want . . . to know both. They don't want to just
hear one side. . . . When they're asking me [what I am] it's
because they want to know, "What kind of Asian are you?
And what else?" So if I say, well . . . if I start out with, "I'm

Mexican," people, number one, will just [say] . . . "Yeah, right." And I think that bothers me, 'cause why would anyone lie about this? Why would I make that up? [Yvonne Garcia]

I would say . . . well, depending on who I was talking to— [If] I'm assuming that they're . . . black, I would say "My mom's black [and] my dad's white." I might say that because "So, what are you?" implies "Are you mixed?" Like that kind of puzzled look that I can imagine on [someone's] face. . . . Leave it at that . . . just because it explains it . . . clarifies which [parent] was white, which one was black. [Donna Tesh]

Some people will just be, "I know you're mixed. What are you mixed with?" And I'll be, "My mother's basically white, my father's basically black. . . . On a general level, that's what it is. You want me to get deeper, that's different. But basically, on that level, I'm black and white, for you." [Alex Bell]

I think for people who are Japanese American I take a little bit more time because it is something I . . . somewhat identify with. [The] Japanese American community . . . there's now a lot of mixed Japanese and white marriages. Out-marriage is a big thing, so I talk about my dad and then it always moves to like what generation are you, because that's another big thing in Japanese American community. [Kay Meki]

As Donna and Kay point out, the background of the inquirer can also influence the particular response a person offers to the question. As discussed in the previous section on "claiming," Prakash adjusts his response according to the inquirer's relative group membership and possible motive for asking the question:

I usually say I'm half Indian, half Croatian and German . . . I say Indian first, because that's what I identify with the most. But Indian, Croatian and German. . . . If somebody who's Indian asked me I would say Indian because that's, a lot of times, what they're looking for. They're trying to determine if I'm Indian. . . . In India there's a real identification with regions, too, so that's really important in terms of language, in terms of how you identify yourself. [Prakash Moghadam]

Sandy similarly adjusts her response to meet the demands of the inquirer:

> Have you ever had someone you don't know . . . ask you about your ethnic heritage? [KW]
>
> Yeah, just because of my last name. They would ask me where it's from. Grocery clerks, random people. It doesn't bother me. [And] my eyes, a few people have commented on my eyes and said "Where are you from? You have interesting eyes."
>
> What do you usually say? [KW]
>
> Iran, I'm Persian. They go "I knew it was something, your eyes." [Sandy Zubaida]

Sandy generally blends in with other whites, but her eyes and last name are sometimes read as ambiguous or foreign. Although she usually identifies as both white and Persian, this example shows how she will match her response (Persian) to the interest of the inquirer (read "What are you? You can't be [just] white.").

A few of the students say the "What are you?" question can be framed as an ultimatum for choosing one side of their heritage over the other, as Alex describes:

> I don't know the exact circumstances, but I do recall someone asking me, "Are you black or white, dude?" I said, "What are you talking about?" And he's all, "You have to be one or the other, dude. Are you black or white?" And I was, like, "I'm both." . . . I don't know why that came about, I just remember someone asking me that. . . . Maybe it's because they're one [race] and they think that somebody else has to be like that. I really don't know what spurs somebody on to ask such a question. 'cause I would never push it upon somebody—that you have to be one [race or another]. If I were to ask somebody, "How would you classify yourself?" . . . I would give my opinion. And [say], "But I want to know what you are really out of curiosity." I'm never going to say "Oh, you have to be one. . . . You can't be that and that at the same time." You know? . . . I don't really know why somebody would do that. [Alex Bell]

Alex was offended that someone would ask him to choose one heritage over another, and quite accurately suggests that it probably stemmed the other person's assumptions about racial identity. This type of interaction provides Alex with more information about how the racial ecology works, and how his mixed heritage is perceived within it.

Several students feel that the "What are you?" question is guided by the stereotype of mixed heritage people as exotic, foreign, attractive, or otherwise unusual in physical appearance. Kris points out that people's comments about her looks are usually positive because they are seen as exotic:

> Sometimes I get the impression that it's some kind of exotic thing and they are just curious, you know "What are you?" . . . Even [by] instructors here [on campus] . . . "What are your parents? Where are your parents from?" . . . Like they don't know the answer . . . [and] they're just trying to figure it out. . . . I think [it's] the exotic thing. I've definitely got comments like "Oh, what an interesting mix." Or "What a nice color." . . . You know, a positive comment on my [appearance]. [Kris Dawson]

Other students express how such comments that highlight their unusual or beautiful appearance make them feel objectified:

> [My] response can be varied depending on who I'm talking to and my mood. . . . So if it it's like . . . they're trying to be so down and . . . if they are taking it as . . . "Oh, you're so exotic!" then it's like "I'm sorry, [it's] not really any of your business!" . . . I try to get out of the situation as soon as possible [when] it comes up and there's no other reason for them to be talking to me [except] they think it's so interesting, something like that. [Kay Meki]

> The other day I was in this workshop . . . and [someone] said to me, "One of the other participants tells me you're Indian and Swiss." And then he said "Oh, I have to say that looks really attractive on you." And I was . . . getting ready to set up for class, I was the assistant for this professor. . . . I just thought, "Okay, I'm going to wait because we're going to get into this when I do my presentation [on individuals of mixed heritage]." . . . I think it comes up, probably, on a daily basis. [Jocelyn Saghal]

Kay, Jocelyn, and other students feel that such overt attention or appraisals of their physical appearance is unwelcome and affects how they respond to the "What are you?" question.

When asked how they would hypothetically respond to a question about their race, all of the students say they would identify with both heritage communities. For some, this answer it is a matter of fact:

> I would say that I am half Persian and half . . . American. I was born in Iran but I was, for all my life that I can remember, raised here. So I call myself an American. [Sandy Zubaida]

> Do I have to pick one? [Alex Bell]

> No, your own words. [KW]

> Oh, okay . . . I'd basically tell them, I be, "Well, my father's African American and my mother is a white lady." So . . . basically, I'm mixed. And go from there. Tell them I'm from a mixed racial background. . . . Most times I find myself being and acting . . . more black. But I'm not going to dismiss being . . . my mother being white. I'm not going to dismiss that part of me. But if somebody asked me, "Do you think you're black or white?" I would be, "What are you talking about? I'm both." "Then why do you act so black? Why can't you act white?" I be all, "Well, that's the way I've grown up." [Alex Bell]

Donna explains why she alternately identifies as just black, or as black (Central American) and white (Dutch American):

> Like I said, I identify myself as black and no problem with that . . . I rather enjoy that. But I think . . . because you can't escape the fact of what I look like, definitely mixed . . . I think that should be represented some way as well. [Donna Tesh]

While she realizes that she is seen as a person of color in the United States, Donna nonetheless realizes that her fair skin, blue eyes, and light hair is seen as representative of her mixed heritage.

Three of the students in this study say they rarely or never encounter the "What are you?" question. This group includes the students who are more generationally distant from their racial minority heritage (and more racially white), as well as one first generation student. Steve, who is first generation black–white, explains:

[My friends] just ask me, "I didn't know that you're mixed?" And I tell them "Yeah, I am." No problem. [Steve Billings]

What do you think they think you are? [KW]

White. [Steve Billings]

Melanie Newheim, who is three-quarters white and one-quarter Mexican American, is rarely asked about her ethnoracial heritage:

> Even though I have . . . a quarter Hispanic in me . . . it's not recognized. . . . People . . . don't really think of me [as Hispanic]. I mean . . . 'cause I'm so white-looking. . . . No, I've never had someone [ask me what I was]. . . . I think maybe . . . one time when that kid saw my mom and then it was, like, "Whoa! You're Mexican?" [Then] I guess some people don't see me just as a white . . . [and] can see Hispanic in me. [Melanie Newheim]

Karen Loomis, who is third generation white–Native American Indian, says she is never asked the "What are you?" question:

> Do people ever . . . ask you about your ethnic or racial background? [KW]
>
> Not really, no. . . . I don't look Native American . . . I think a lot of people think of me as a white person. [Karen Loomis]

Of all the students in the study, these three are the only ones whose physical appearance and racial background are not called into question by outsiders.

The common thread running through these encounters with the "What are you?" question is the racial ambiguity of the students, whether it is suggested by physical appearance alone or in conjunction with their names. These interactions provide students with critical information about the nature of race and mixed race in U.S. society. For example, most of these mixed heritage students learn that their physical appearance is considered unusual within the racial ecology and suggestive of their mixed heritage. The women in particular are prone to unwarranted appraisals of their physical appearance and come to realize how their looks symbolize an "exoticness" that is valued in society. By the time they reach college age, students seem to expect these types of questions and some begin to craft varying responses depending on the identity and motivation of the inquirer.

SUMMARY

Most of the students share a common experience of marginalization within their heritage communities because of factors associated with their mixed background. Physical appearance, dissimilar interactional styles, and even the fact of dual heritage can stigmatize the mixed heritage person as foreign and culturally suspect, or even simply invisible to other group members. Because their cultural legitimacy and loyalty are in question as a result of these markers, mixed individuals are frequently assigned a liminal, or marginal, status in the community. A community's attitudes toward out-marriage, as well as their historical relations with other groups, are mediating factors that affect the status accorded mixed heritage people. As a result, these students often learn to consciously or unconsciously adapt to the cultural context of the community in order to achieve a more full citizenship within the group.

Similar to ethnic identity, student approaches to racial identity differ in emphasis. Alex, Donna, Jocelyn, Kay, Marta, Prakash, and Yvonne place a strong emphasis on their minority heritage, while the other students place equal emphasis on their dual heritage.[4] Despite these varying degrees of emphasis, however, none of the students prefers to identify with only one heritage community at all times. Self-identification varies across contexts, even for those students who strongly identify as racial minorities. This may be due to the fact that racial identity, unlike ethnic identity, is seen as more of an objective fact of birth. It may also be the result of students' lived racial experiences that, for some, means being seen as a minority within both heritage communities. The next chapter will explore these trends more thoroughly.

Characterized by spatial imagery (e.g., margins, middle ground, bridges, etc.), students' discourses about race are directly informed by their experiences transgressing traditional racial boundaries. The findings suggest that these experiences encourage recently mixed individuals to construct an interracial lens for interpreting their racial heritage and/or identity. Shifting labels of identification, challenging peer assumptions about their identity, and bucking racial norms of classification provide evidence of a nontraditional identity approach for these individuals born and raised in the borderlands of race. The following chapter will examine how students understand their experiences as individuals of mixed heritage in the United States.

NOTES

1. However, Chapter 6 will discuss how first generation students of part-white ancestry are often accorded a unique ethnoracial status by whites who see them as more white than "x" (e.g., black, Asian, etc.).

2. It should also be noted here that of the thirteen part-white students, only five are nonwhite in phenotype and they often are seen as racially ambiguous; the other eight students readily are viewed as white.

3. Steve Billings is the only student who says he has never been asked this question, most likely because people assume he is white.

4. For Yvonne, the emphasis is toward her Mexican American heritage rather than her Japanese American heritage. Some would argue that within our collective racial hierarchy, Latinos occupy a more subordinate positions to Asians. Kris Dawson, however, is the one student who does not adopt an interracial frame of reference from an egalitarian standpoint. Instead, it is the result of an ascribed African American status in society. This will be explored further in the next chapter.

Chapter 6

On Being Mixed: Issues and Interpretations

There's advantages and there's disadvantages to being mixed. . . . On one end . . . some white people that won't accept black people will accept you just because . . . they'll be "Oh, he's white, he's white." And there's black people who'll be, "No, he's just black." You know? But the disadvantages would be, at the same time, some black people [will say], "Well, you white." . . . And there's some white people who be, "You black. We don't want you." . . . I mean, there's advantages and disadvantages.

Alex Bell

It's not easy shifting . . . [into] the mainstream . . . community. . . . This is frustrating for me. . . . In my heart I think there are other places. . . . [It] is part of my culture, [but] it's so tiring because they don't necessarily see me as part of their culture.

Kay Meki

In Chapters 3, 4, and 5, I examine the many facets of ethnic and racial-identity development among this group of mixed heritage students. This chapter presents students' perspectives on being mixed by considering the meaning students confer to their experiences as individuals with interracial/ethnic heritage. As you have seen in prior chapters, the students in this study come from a wide range of backgrounds and have very diverse experiences. Alex's statement at the start of this chapter, for example, is just one perspective of many on what it means to be mixed.

While the orientations students take toward their ethnoracial identities vary, there are several common threads that tie them together. Most of the students describe their ethnic and racial experiences as characterized by mobility. This is true particularly among the first-generation students who emphasize the significance of having to negotiate group boundaries when traveling between heritage communities. As a result of migrating between heritage communities, many mixed heritage students learn to discern and adapt to the cultural norms of each group. Yet mixed heritage students frequently are subjected to marginalization within one or both heritage communities because of their dual ancestry and cultural experiences. Students describe how, to varying degrees, being mixed means they face suspicion, hostility, and other marginalizing reactions within the community as their legitimacy and loyalty are tested across new contexts.

Students also say migrating between heritage communities helps them to nourish and honor their cultural roots. This appreciation of one's diverse roots is particularly important for first-generation students who aspire to establish a sense of balance toward both heritage communities via their self-identification. Thus, the labels that mixed heritage students use to self-identify are guided by an egalitarian ethic. These labels shift across contexts in a way that allows students to stay true to their experience and heritage. For some, a symbolic identification with both heritage communities is the only way they can realize a balanced approach to their identity in light of a lived experience that is more asymmetrical. The fluid nature of students' self-identification strategies suggests a transgressive quality, too. All of the students in this study self-identify in dynamic and/or open-ended ways that defy rigid standards of group membership and challenge linear identity models. Like their trail-blazing parents, mixed heritage students are in their own way transgressing the ethnic and racial borders by refusing to be identified with only one group at all times.

The experiences of mixed heritage students often lead them to adopt a particular attitude toward ethnic and race relations. Some see themselves as bridges across their heritage communities. Many feel they understand different perspectives more readily than most or are more likely to reject exclusionary and ethnocentric attitudes. Such commonly held perceptions among the majority of the students in this study support prior data that show mixed heritage individuals exhibit higher levels of cognitive flexibility than most single heritage people.

Finally, mixed heritage students see themselves and their experiences as unique. Many students note how they grew up in isolation from other individuals of recently mixed heritage, thus creating an aura of solitude and distinctiveness around the experience. While mixed heritage individuals do not constitute a traditional group (based on a common ancestry or place of origin, language, culture, phenotype, worldview, or history) their multiple heritage and nontraditional ethnoracial experiences do constitute a common ground. Ultimately, these mixed heritage students prefer to identify not with each other as a group, but with their relative heritage communities.

BORDER NEGOTIATIONS

As outlined in Chapter 1, after completing the Expressive Autobiographic Interview each participant was shown a series of four visuals. The visuals represent four possible ways of managing social borders, in this case, of race and ethnicity. It was stressed that each visual represents a positive strategy for negotiating the boundaries of one's heritage communities. After giving a brief introduction to each visual, students were informed that they might not find any appropriate for describing their experiences, or that one, more than one, or all the visuals may be somehow relevant.

Surprisingly, all the subjects identified with at least one visual, and fourteen out of fifteen identified with at least two. The visuals are titled as follows: Home Base/Visitor's Base; Life on the Border; Both Feet in Both Worlds; and Shifting Identity Gears (see Figures 1.1–1.4). The visuals are computer-generated and feature gender-neutral stick figures. Below I provide an overview of the visuals and the findings from each of the four visuals.

Home Base/Visitor's Base

In this visual, the mixed heritage person is illustrated as grounded mostly in one community of heritage, while interactions with the other community occur through occasional visits to this other "base." The frequency of these trips to the "visitor's base" may vary greatly, and a person may find that their home and visitor's bases switch over time.

The Home Base/Visitor's Base visual implies the mobility a person may experience as they interact within two heritage communities. A striking eleven out of fifteen students selected this visual; of these were eight of the nine university students and three of the six high school students.[1] Among the part-white students, Sandy, Karen, and Melanie tend to identify symbolically with the Home

Base visual. These three students do not describe any sustained participation within their minority communities of heritage, mostly due to local population ratios and generational distance.

Donna and Kris discuss why they found the Home Base visual to be particularly resonant of their experiences:

> Home Base strikes a chord with me just because where I consider home is probably the white community. That [visual] I see as my home base. So I guess the racial community that is white [is my home base], pretty much. [Donna Tesh]

> This [Home Base visual] works for me. I sort of feel like I'm basically anchored within the white community, and that I kind of have ties to the black community. . . . I still interact with [the black community] at times, but not predominantly. [Kris Dawson]

Yvonne is careful to point out how living more in one community does not affect how she feels about her other community of heritage:

> This [Home Base visual] . . . probably sounds the most like me, because I'm mostly into my Mexican side . . . I would say . . . really the only other times that I even sort of, maybe go over to the other [Japanese American] side would be when I'm in Hawaii. . . . And just like you said, it's not . . . a bad thing, but it's just more on the back burner 'cause I don't have that contact here. [Yvonne Garcia]

As Yvonne articulates so well, geographical distance from a heritage community does not necessarily mean a person devalues that community, it might merely be a reflection of their current situation (such as attending a predominantly white institution).

These quotes highlight, once again, the role of geographical distance within the identity-development process. Sandy also says her mainstream experience is the most immediate and, thus, the more influential on her sense of identity:

> I'd say [Home Base is] pretty accurate. . . . But I don't see it switching for me, unless I want to live in Iran. I don't know . . . I've been here my whole life (well since I was four) surrounded by this culture. . . . You never know . . . what's going to happen. And . . . I suppose ten years down the line I could be living in Iran and surrounded by Per-

sians . . . I don't know, I don't see that happening. [Sandy Zubaida]

Like some of the other students, distance is quite literal in Sandy's case, although there are parts of the United States with higher concentrations of Iranian Americans. Still, as Sandy mentions in an earlier chapter, the distance between California and Iran is not only geographical, it is also political since she does not truly have the option of returning to Iran because of the current political situation. For several other students, having the choice to visit one's heritage community may depend on socioeconomic factors, as Jocelyn Saghal's comments underscore "I was just thinking. . . . This is where I live and where I've grown up most of my life. . . . But . . . I traveled back and forth [between California, Switzerland, and India]."

Marta's interpretation of Home Base/Visitor's Base reveals how being mixed carries a risk of marginalization:

> It must be [Home Base/Visitor's Base]. Because when I have my choice in the matter, I surround myself with Latino community. . . . But there's not always . . . a very large Latino [population], so I have no choice and I can't [always] participate with that community. . . . And so I have to switch . . . I guess it's a switching. And right now in (this is why this traveling [image] was kind of attractive) I feel like this particular group of Latinos [at school] . . . is isolating itself from a larger group somehow. And I don't buy into that. As much as I want to be part of the Latino community and feel associated with the Latino community, I don't appreciate the isolating [tendency] because it only . . . brings up antagonism that I don't think is necessary. . . . I feel like I don't belong, like I very easily float across both of those borders. And I wonder if I'm paying for it and that's why I'm feeling more outside the Latino community now. But that's not how I normally feel. [Pointing to the visual] that's why I don't feel like there's any balance. . . . Because I'll associate . . . across the board with anyone, anyone who makes me feel comfortable. Although my preference . . . my interests are with the Latino community. [Marta Elizondo]

Marta suggests that her experiences living in predominantly white settings and being able to "float across . . . borders" may contribute to her marginalization within this group of Latinas. The Home Base visual helps Marta to explain how her circumstances are not by choice or ideal, and should not be held against her by her peers with whom she identifies so strongly.

Eight of the eleven students who selected the Home Base visual also chose the Shifting Identity Gears visual. This suggests that many students see themselves as migrating between communities and adjusting their behavior to match the context.

Life on the Border

The Life on the Border visual depicts a person sitting cross-legged at the point where two communities converge. This particular orientation, as Root (1996) notes, may resonate for the person who sees a universality to the human experience, as well as someone who views their own identity essentially mixed or multifaceted.

Six students selected this visual, representing half of the high school students and one-third of the university students. Both Sheila and Amanda describe the Life on the Border as analogous to a bridge experience. For Sheila, it means having access to both of her communities of heritage:

> I think I'd go with, generally [Both Feet In Both Worlds] and [Life on the Border] . . . I know what I am, and I actually like that. . . . And I get to know each half of my ethnicity. . . . I usually don't let it factor too big on each day. I know what I am, and if anyone asks me about it, I'll be glad to tell them. [Sheila Rafkin]

Amanda Wilson says, "I guess this one, [Life on the Border], then. Because I'm going to relate to both sides through being Christian." Like Sheila, Amanda relates to the Life on the Border visual because it depicts a way of connecting with both communities equally.

Melanie, who is second-generation mixed heritage, proposes an interesting alteration to the Life on the Border visual, explaining, "Maybe with just my hand . . . touching the other one. Sitting [more] on one side and touching [the other side]. . . . Just . . . knowing that it's there." This suggestion stems from Melanie's generational distance from the Latino community and her grounding in the mainstream. Melanie's experiences are not as balanced as in the visual; her desire to keep in touch with the Latino community reflects her more symbolic orientation toward this side of her heritage.

Some students point out that they have no choice but to see themselves as poised between the two communities. Kay says this position at the border is not voluntary:

I also feel that sometimes I am on the border. . . . Not the way that I perceive my identity, but how others perceive me. They sometimes put me on the border. . . . I know I've changed myself . . . I think growing up [I thought] "Yeah, I'm right here [on the border]." . . . This was always the case, but I didn't know how to talk about it. [Kay Meki]

For Kay, Life on the Border is the result of how others see her, as not quite Japanese nor white but somewhere in the middle. Kay also feels her self-perceptions have changed over time. Donna, too, sees Life on the Border as an orientation that results from being ascribed a liminal status by both groups:

This [Life] on the Border because, especially like we were talking about the college atmosphere. It's hard to involve yourself in one [group] without [isolating] from the other. . . . I like to be a person who likes to be involved with more than one thing . . . I think 'cause of familial [issues . . . like being] the mediator. . . . I think that's the role that I play. [Donna Tesh]

Donna believes her experiences at home contribute to her wanting to mediate between her heritage communities and not socialize within just one or the other, at least at school.

Three high school students, compared with one university student, describe Life on the Border as reflective of a bridge experience, which suggests a developmental dimension. Two college students think this position at the border is the result of being placed in the middle between two groups, while the high school students see it as an interpretation of their identities. This may be due to the greater sense of polarization students feel when attending college versus at the high school level. It would be instructive to use this visual among a larger sample of high school and university students to see if this finding does correlate with age and college attendance.

Both Feet in Both Worlds

The Both Feet in Both Worlds visual shows an individual whose two feet are positioned within both communities of heritage. This person is not split between two worlds, but is firmly grounded in both worlds at the same time. Five of the fifteen selected this visual, four of whom are high school students. Alex Bell describes the Both Feet visual as representative of his holistic approach identity:

[I like the visual] because . . . I don't necessarily choose
one or the other . . . I just, basically, come across as Alex,
you know? If you ask me "Who are you?" or "What are you?"
I'm going to be, "I'm human, I'm Alex, you know? I'm not
going to be black, I'm not going to be white, I'm just Alex."
I mean, if you have to have a description, I s'pose I'm going
to [be] . . . right there [with Both Feet in Both Worlds].
[Alex Bell]

Alex has an uncompromising sense of identity as both black and
white, not one or the other, even though he does identify ethnically
as black. The different strands of his identity can't be teased apart;
black, white, and "human, I'm Alex." The one college student, Sandy,
says, "I guess that's one of my feet? . . . It's more in one than the
other, but yeah, I'd say they were both in." Although she feels connected to both communities, Sandy doesn't see herself as being on
equal footing in both groups. She suggests an alteration similar to
Melanie's that could convey varying depths of grounding in a heritage community.

Karen mentions the benefits of having Both Feet in Both Worlds:

I like being Native American I think better than saying I'm
white. Only because . . . everybody says that they're white,
or they're Irish, or they're Scottish. . . . There are so many
people like that, and there aren't very many people who are
Native American. Or at least if they are they don't . . . ever
know what they are. So I guess that I like to take the opportunity to use it every time I can . . . my three sixty-
fourths [Native American ancestry]. [Karen Loomis]

Karen, who is third generation, clearly sees her Native American
heritage as an attractive, exotic option within a mainstream context. Also referring to flexibility, Steve Billings says he likes the
visual " 'cause Both Feet In is like I'm already there, and I could do
whatever . . . I have like an easier time trying to get in where I fit
in." Here and in other parts of his interview, Steve describes the
sense of freedom and connection he feels from being able to participate in both of his heritage communities.

Kay and Marta comment on how the Both Feet in Both Worlds is
an idealistic representation for them:

[Both Feet in Both Worlds] is my perfect world. But I don't
think that both my communities are on equal footing. . . .
The ideal is there for me. [Kay Meki]

I don't feel like it's . . . [Both Feet In] because I don't feel
I'm completely grounded in both. There are times when I
feel comfortable in both and uncomfortable in both. . . .
[The visual] makes me feel like I'm supposed to be com-
fortable in both and I don't feel like it's that. [Marta
Elizondo]

Both university students, Kay and Marta view Both Feet in Both
Worlds as an unrealistic depiction of their experiences. Like the
Life on the Border visual, the attractiveness of the Both Feet visual to high school students suggests a developmental dimension
to the identification process as they adopt a more utopian approach
to their self-identification.

Shifting Identity Gears

The Shifting Identity Gears visual portrays parts of an individual's
identity shifting into the foreground, while other parts shift into
the background as the person moves across social contexts. Interestingly, all the students who identified with the Shifting Identity
Gears visual also selected the Home Base/Visitor's Base visual; both
depict an experience of active movement between two worlds. The
Shifting Gears visual suggests that one's identity can be situational;
as a person crosses into a new setting, different facets of his or her
identity are brought into the fore to meet the interactional demands
of the situation. Nine of the fifteen participants find this visual
helpful for describing their experiences, two of whom are high school
students.

Jocelyn, Donna, and Kris all see themselves shifting gears to
adjust to the rules of the cultural context:

The Indian comes out more . . . certain things com[e] out
more at certain times with certain people in certain situations. [Jocelyn Saghal]

Shifting Gears—definitely it's all the time . . . [both] consciously or unconsciously. [Donna Tesh]

I definitely see myself sort of putting on different hats at
times. [Kris Dawson]

"Putting on different hats," as Kris calls it, seems to be a common
practice among university students. Although she identifies with the
Shifting Gears visual, Sandy does not feel she does it very frequently:

This one I can see . . . [Shifting Identity Gears] somewhat.
But I think I'm pretty much [in the same] context. It's clear
that my life is pretty much grounded in [mainstream] society. But I do enjoy being in Persian culture and learning
about it . . . seeing it. . . . But in my day-to-day life, it's not
common [to shift gears]. [Sandy Zubaida]

Kay describes shifting gears but not being recognized as a legitimate group member:

Probably "Shifting Gears" . . . [I'm] primarily based in one
[community] and moving to the other. And now I'm finding [that] I'm here [in a mainstream context] . . . but it's not
easy shifting . . . [into] the mainstream . . . community. . . .
This is frustrating for me—that that's where I am. In my
heart I think there are other places. . . . It's also strange
because when you're mixed, you know you are also European American. . . . [And] "Hello grad school!"—it's all white
culture. . . . I remember the first few days I was talking to
my other friend, she's Korean and European–Polish American. And she's said "I'm so tired, I've been schmoozing all
day. I can't do it. I feel so fake—they have no idea who I
am. I'm just playing the white game," or something. And
that is part of my culture, [but] it's so tiring because they
don't necessarily see me as part of their culture. [Kay Meki]

While the frequency of shifting gears varies by student, these comments show how mixed heritage students develop an awareness of
the different cultural demands between their communities, including the mainstream. Kay recognizes that her educational choices
have placed her squarely in the culture of the mainstream on a
daily basis. Although she sees herself as white, too, Kay says not
being seen as white gets tiring. And being in a predominantly white
community is frustrating for her because her sense of connection to
the Japanese American community is carried with her at all times,
or as she explains, "In my heart I think there are other places."

When discussing how gears are shifted, Missy, Yvonne, and
Prakash each mention altering their speech patterns:

If I'm in a certain place . . . that part will come out in me
and will show up. And if I'm with my Italian friends it will
also show, and I'll start talking like they will. Or I'll be
talking regularly when I'm with my other friends . . . I'll

get the different [way of] speaking, [the] language, and I'll have to knock it out of me when I . . . [leave]. [Missy Connor]

[Shifting Identity Gears] sounded like me for a little while, 'cause you said that sometimes you bring it to the forefront a little bit more. . . . That sounded like me. I think . . . sometimes it depends on who I'm talking to. You know, you change the way you talk. [Yvonne Garcia]

It's a combination of these [Home Base and Shifting Gears visuals]. If I'm in this [Home] situation, this is the Indian community, the one I'm surrounded by. And then moving in and out of Croatian community, but also moving in and out of a middle-class Catholic background. That same kind of shifting . . . like I'll speak . . . my manner of speech is different with my mom's side of the family. My speech is different with my black friends, too. I talk differently with my friends from Chicago than with my friends from New York. [Prakash Moghadam]

These accounts are similar to Marta's comment in a previous chapter, where she describes her unconscious ability for empathetic listening by changing the way she talks to match the style of her interlocutor. Although he identifies with the Shifting Gears visual, there are negative connotations for Alex:

For myself, it's basically . . . different circumstances, different situations reflect on how you're going to act. . . . And that's why I'll pick that [visual], because, you know, I do switch. It's not necessarily something I enjoy doing. But, I do do it, either way. [Alex Bell]

For Alex, changing the way he acts generally means acting white. He mentions elsewhere how his preferred interactional style as a black person has been the source of ridicule, so shifting gears was a necessary, but not desirable means of survival in a mainstream context.

Finally, Alex makes an interesting point about the border negotiation visuals in general:

See, it's kind of hard for me to pick either one [of the visuals], any of them, because I don't want to. But I know that that's the way it is. [Alex Bell]

Any of the (visuals), or any of your heritage communities?
[KW]

Any . . . both. [Alex Bell]

You don't have to pick (any of the visuals). [KW]

Oh, I know I don't have to. But I mean, in reality I would
be those [Both Feet in Both Worlds and Shifting Identity
Gears]. . . . What I'm saying [is], if it was up to me, I wouldn't
choose. . . . That's the way it is, but . . . I don't feel that I
should have to be in the middle . . . or I don't feel I should
have to switch. . . . And I feel real bad when people [say]
you have to switch . . . or . . . "Okay, you're with us now and
. . . we just act a certain way." . . . It's real sad that . . . as
far as this world has come, it's still at that [point]. . . . It's
just real sad. But . . . the fact of the matter is that things
are the way they are. . . . They're not necessarily correct,
but they [just] are, regardless. So . . . I would pick [Both
Feet and Shifting Gears].

While all of the students say they find the visuals helpful, Alex
laments the fact that some people are put in the middle or pressured to act a certain way. He thinks it is unfortunate that he can't
just be himself; instead, he must negotiate how he presents himself and his identity as do many of the mixed heritage students in
this study.

THOUGHTS ON ETHNORACIAL IDENTITY

Several interview questions target how students see themselves
as individuals of mixed heritage. The following section explores their
thoughts about ethnoracial identity, encounters with race/ethnicity
surveys, and perceptions of their future children's identities.

Dynamic Identities

Self-Perception

The constancy of students' ethnoracial identities was assessed
through their responses to other probes, as well as to those following:

• Do you ever feel more, or see yourself as more [X ethnoracial heritage]
  sometimes? Can you give me an example?

• Do you ever feel more, or see yourself as more [Y ethnoracial heritage] sometimes? Can you give me an example?

Six students (Marta, Steve, Yvonne, Amanda, Prakash, and Donna) describe "feeling like" a member of one heritage community and not the other. Amanda and Prakash don't know how it feels to be anything other than Chinese American and Indian American, respectively, while both Steve and Donna remark that they don't know what it feels like to be white. Marta and Yvonne point out that how they look can be at odds with how they identify:

> I always feel more Mexican American, even though I might feel like I'm being looked at some more [because of my appearance]. But inside I always feel more Mexican American than white. [Marta Elizondo]

> I [feel] Mexican . . . I think that's just probably the way that I feel in general. . . . I don't look Mexican, but I would say . . . I feel Mexican. I don't really think about myself in any other way. . . . I don't know what it feels like to be Asian American in the United States because I haven't had that experience. [Yvonne Garcia]

Despite their appearance, Marta and Yvonne cannot say that they recall a time when they felt white or Japanese American, respectively.

By contrast, eight students say they feel like members of both communities of heritage, although at different times. Alex, Missy, Sandy, Sheila, Jocelyn, Melanie, Kris, and Kay all believe different contexts bring out different aspects of their identities. Alex says he finds himself in a black mode most of the time, but he does slide into a more white mode on occasion. Spending time in Japan led Kay to reflect on this process:

> I think living in Japan I went through some weird things over there. I think I felt American, definitely. . . . Realizing how much as Americans . . . [our] mainstream culture is sort of white culture. But what does that mean then? . . . What have we internalized to be our American identity? So for me it's always so weird . . . I have a lot of family [in Japan]. . . . So while they're seeing me as an American, I'm trying to get more access to my Japanese roots, kind of thing. So that was a big tension. At the same time, I'm realizing the things that I crave [is] missing my Americanness, [which] is so linked to white America. So that was

really weird to deal with all of those things at the same
time. [Kay Meki]

Being in Japan made Kay how "white" she felt in that environment. Only Karen who is third generation mixed heritage says she
never notices feeling white or Native American, most likely because
she has been raised solely in a mainstream context with no lasting
connections with her minority heritage.

Self-Identification

After being asked about these probes, students were asked the
following:

- Would there ever be a time when you would identify solely as [a member of X ethnoracial group of heritage]? Can you give me an example? or
  why not?
- Would there ever be a time when you would identify solely as [a member of Y ethnoracial group of heritage]? Can you give me an example? or
  why not?

Quite surprisingly, despite these findings, not one student said
he or she identifies as a member of only one ethnoracial group at
all times and across all contexts. Eight students (Alex, Amanda,
Sandy, Sheila, Steve, Missy, Kris, and Jocelyn) say they identify
with both groups of heritage, or as mixed, or as some other desig-
nation connoting their dual heritage. Usually, students explain this
choice of identification as simply a reflection of reality, as Steve
and Missy illustrate:

> I would probably say black and white. Because it's who I
> am, it's who I want to be. [Steve Billings]

> Because that's mostly what I am. I'm half Indian, so that . . .
> takes up half of me. And the other . . . half . . . is European . . .
> it's really weird that way. [Missy Connor]

For Kris, however, her identification as both black and white seems
similarly factual, but in a different way:

> I usually just say I'm half black, half white. I think part of
> it is trying to reject the feeling that I'm all black. I mean . . .
> I'm definitely white in certain ways. My mom is white and
> I grew up with her, and so I just feel like I have to not

ignore that part of myself. . . . In all of those sort of outwardly appearance kind of ways, languages or appearance . . . mannerisms, things like that . . . I think I want to strive for [being seen as more white]. Especially if they're strangers, [not] seeing me [as] nonthreatening . . . [not] an aggressive speaking [person, someone who] they would sort of fear . . . sort of angry. . . . Part of it's . . . I want to fit into the white community, too. So I don't like to rock the boat. . . . I think part of it is that the way I've really rejected being black because of the things that I see in the media and my own impressions of the black community as a whole. . . . It's not really wanting to be associated—you know—to have strangers associate me with those characteristics. So I think that's why I act white . . . to give strangers an assumption that I'm not one of *those* type blacks. . . . I think that . . . that's more comfortable for me. [Kris Dawson]

Kris speaks to the tension between feeling more ethnically white and being seen as "just black." Her cultural experiences living with her white mother in predominantly white settings understandably lead Kris to identify ethnically as white. But Kris makes it painfully clear that she values things that are associated with European American culture, and devalues things associated with black culture (presented here through stereotypes of black people as threatening, aggressive, and angry). Kris's physical appearance causes others to "ignore that part" of her, the white part, and she therefore feels the need to push her whiteness out.

Kris's comments show a heightened concern about how she is seen by others and reveals an internalization of racist, mainstream stereotypes about African Americans. Among this group of fifteen students, Kris is the only person who conveys any internalized racism and bias toward a heritage community. In other parts of her interview, Kris reveals how her ideas about whiteness are bound up in notions of socioeconomic status and privilege (unmarked by race), while her understandings of blackness are described in terms of disadvantage and pathology (marked by culture and race). When she compares herself to the few black peers she had growing up, Kris describes them in consistently negative terms, as coming from working class backgrounds and associating them with truancy, drug abuse, and unwed motherhood. And while Kris interprets her mother's physical abuse to be the result of her financial stress as a working-class single parent, she explains her father's physical abuse as the result of his African American culture or race. The emotional abuse experienced by Kris and her sister when he abducted them for two years, as well as the physical abuse they witnessed toward his two wives at that time, may have played a critical part in how she learned to view the black community.

Finally, seven students say that how they identify largely depends on the context in which they find themselves. Donna, Sandy, Marta, Yvonne, Karen, Prakash, and Melanie all describe shifting their self-identification depending on the person with whom they're interacting. As mentioned in Chapter 5, Yvonne and Donna both say that how they identify in person is influenced by their ambiguous phenotype:

> I always say that I'm half Japanese and half Mexican. . . . Only recently . . . I've given up Chicana. . . . But I don't always say that because people . . . want to know both. They don't want to just hear one side. [Yvonne Garcia]

> I identify myself as black . . . [but] depending on who I was talking to, I would say "My mom's black my dad's white." I might say that because "So what are you?" implies the . . . question, "Are you mixed?" [Donna Tesh]

And even though Marta feels ethnically Mexican American at all times, her self-identification does not always match:

> When I go dancing, this always happens . . . [I get asked] "Where are you from?" [which] usually means "What country are you from?" . . . I say I was born in San Jose, [they say] "Well where are your parents from, then?" . . . It's always a difficult question for me to answer because I know they want to know where my Latinoness comes. . . . So I usually go with my grandparents, my dad's parents, and say that they were from Mexico. . . . And every once in awhile, but not as often, I will . . . say that I'm also Italian German, that my grandfather was born in Italy. And I always make a comment how . . . I'm all mixed up, or whatever. . . . It's very hard to answer that question. . . . My immediate reaction is to want to say "I'm Latina," but I don't want to cut out the other side of me, either. . . . Actually . . . I feel like I need to do a lot about the other side of me, too. That I can't let that die, either. [Marta Elizondo]

One of the students who most strongly identifies with one ethnic group, Marta declares that her decision to identify as both Mexican

American and European American seems to stem from a deep respect and pride she feels for her heritage on all sides. She also notes that she has more work to "do" to develop her sense of connection to her Italian and German roots. Kay changes her identification for a different reason, however:

> So if you want to be specific, you say *Nikkei* America-*jiin*, which means of Japanese descent but from America. . . . I also identify with Japanese American, or Japanese American of mixed race. . . . I don't usually identify as mixed in most situations. . . . If I'm hanging out with other people who are mixed . . . then . . . it seems like that's understood. But in most other situations I don't think that that would be understood in the right way . . . I don't know if people are ready to hear [about my experience]. They wouldn't have any context for that. [Kay Meki]

Generally self-identifying as *Nikkei*, Kay does identifies with her mixed heritage when the context allows. Pointing to the misconceptions and stereotypes around identifying as mixed heritage, Kay is most comfortable saying she's mixed only in the company of other mixed individuals who have a framework for understanding the complexities of her experience.

Constancy and Range

Another way students' perceptions about their ethnoracial identities were explored was through two overt questions about the relative constancy of these perceptions. Students were asked the following questions:

- Do you think your ideas about your racial/ethnic identity have changed? If yes, how and why?
- Do you think they will change in the future? Why or why not?

Eight students say that how they see themselves in terms of their heritage have not changed at all. While they may each have different approaches to their identities, Steve, Sheila, Amanda, Alex, Missy, Marta, Karen, and Prakash each say their identities are unchanging. Alex and Prakash explain:

> I feel like I've always felt the same about who I am, and my culture, and so forth. But [when] I was just young . . . I

was, I guess, scared to voice it to people that wouldn't agree with me or wouldn't like . . . me talking about . . . that part of me. But I don't think [my views have] ever changed. Naw. My views of my culture and my ethnic background have never changed. Never have changed. [Alex Bell]

I move in and out . . . depending on what community I'm in. . . . But not in any significant way, I don't think [they've changed . . . my ideas about my identity have stayed] fairly constant, yeah. [Prakash Moghadam]

Interestingly, all the male participants in this study (Alex, Prakash, and Steve) feel their identities have remained static across time, which may suggest a correlation between gender and ethnoracial self-perception.

Seven students feel their sense of ethnoracial identity has changed. Although sometimes incapable of explaining just how, Kris, Yvonne, Kay, Donna, Sandy, Melanie, and Jocelyn all feel their identities have shifted. Many of these students believe in the importance of learning more deeply about the culture of one or both heritage groups. Jocelyn talks about how this learning curve influenced her identity:

When I went to India, it was like "Why wasn't I married and why was I traveling alone?" . . . I was like "Damn straight. I want to be American because I have a right to travel . . . I'm not going to fall prey to this . . . I don't want these expectations placed on me. Because I did not grow up here. . . . I'm here and I'm exploring and I'm finding out a little bit more about me and my father . . . in a really free, enriching, philosophical, intense experience. But I can't be who you really want me to be because I'm not just Indian." That's when I cut my hair really short. They wouldn't cut my hair. . . . I cut my hair, I stopped . . . wearing my Punjabi clothes. I was like "Now . . . I want to look like my values. . . . If I want to wear jeans, I want to wear jeans . . . and don't judge me for it . . . because I'm going to." . . . I went through this really angry phase. And they wouldn't cut my hair. I had to go to . . . five places. I had to go . . . to a five-star hotel and they were "You looked better before." They're very frank, Indians. But I knew that. . . . So I think when I went there, I was like "Oh, yeah, I'm totally Indian." But now, I'm not just totally Indian. [Jocelyn Saghal]

Jocelyn's trip to India was a defining moment; it was through her experiences in the country that she recognized how culturally different she was because of her mixed heritage and U.S. upbringing.

Asked whether how they see themselves will change in the future, only four students believe their identities will not fluctuate. Steve, Amanda, Sheila, and Marta are the four students who say they don't anticipate any movement in their orientations. Marta underscores the importance of her ethnic experience as Mexican American:

> I don't foresee myself ever being involved in the European side of me as I do the Mexican side of me. . . . The Mexican side of me incorporates a lot of pretty deep-set values that the European [doesn't]. And when I say European I'm thinking more [of a] U.S. stereotypical American type . . . I don't know if . . . that's necessarily what my European side of the family subscribes to. In some way I guess . . . they do. Because if I look at my mom's sisters and their families, they're pretty typical white American. . . . There's too much ingrained in me that I could never change to that. I mean, I could never be a sorority person, or be involved with fraternities and that kind of stuff. . . . Again, I see that as kind of [a] white American-type thing. I don't know if I could put all the feelings and values into words. . . . I might subscribe to the Italian part of it because I know that was very family-oriented. . . . That's stereotypical, [but] it sounds like that was what it was like for my mom, but I don't see that as typically American. . . . It is a choice, and I've focused on one side more than the other. . . . I don't know why it has to be a choice, but it seems like it has to be a choice . . . for some reason. Or it's hard to put them together—you can't. I don't know, maybe you can put them together, but I don't see how they come together, do you know what I mean? [Marta Elizondo]

Unlike the other three students, Marta feels her identity is not informed by her European American heritage. While earlier in this section she says she would like to learn more about her German and Italian heritage, Marta largely sees the cultural values of her heritage communities as irreconcilable, making a shift in her identity orientation unlikely.

Eleven students say "yes" or "perhaps" they see their sense of identity changing in the future. Yvonne, Missy, Kris, Karen, Kay, Prakash, Melanie, Jocelyn, Donna, and Sandy suspect they could experience some change. Alex and Jocelyn talk about why:

I can see them changing as far as my identity, but not my heritage. 'Cause I don't think that heritage is something that you can change. . . . The way that I see myself as . . . in respect to race? I don't think that's going to change. I don't think my views on myself are going to change due to race. I think just . . . growth. But as far as my race goes, I'm not going to see myself changing. I might find new words to identify myself. But as far as me being what I am, that's not ever going to change. I'm not ever going to see that any different. [Alex Bell]

I feel pretty solid . . . but . . . I really want to move to Switzerland to get my citizenship. . . . Maybe . . . when I go to Switzerland . . . I'll feel a little more Swiss than I do now. . . . Maybe I'll make peace a little with my mother. . . . It could be a deepening. And I do still want to go back and spend more time [in] India. . . . I would like to be in a lot of different places at a lot of different points in my life. [Jocelyn Saghal]

Alex, Jocelyn, and several other students say there is the potential for developing a deeper sense of connection with one or both heritage groups. For example, Yvonne feels strongly Chicana but does not rule out the possibility of growth on her Japanese American side:

I took this African American psychology class and we learned about this [identity development] model. . . . I think I'm at the point where I'm more . . . neutral. . . . I'm not neutral . . . I'm still more on the Mexican side. But I know that at the end of this sort of model you get to the point where you're just . . . more in the middle. . . . You can understand white people's experience, you can understand your experience. . . . And you're not so adamant. 'cause I know I did go through a little phase of . . . Chicano power . . . I was really into that. And I started leveling off a little bit more . . . I kind of probably think as I get older it might change a little bit. But I don't see myself ever really ever having a different experience. But then it does . . . depend on where you live. . . . If I move to Hawaii, I might all of a sudden consider myself Asian again . . . or something. I don't rule it out, but I doubt it. [Yvonne Garcia]

For some students, further developing a connection with a heritage community (what Jocelyn above calls a "deepening") suggests a simultaneously dynamic yet stable identity development process for many mixed heritage students as their ties can continue to unfold within one or both groups. In this way, identity may continue to be dynamic for students whose identities have always been subject to change, while for others it may move from a stable to a more dynamic orientation over time.

In thinking about how they might change, both Prakash and Donna mention the influence a future spouse may have on their sense of identity:

> [Yes it could change], depending on who I would marry, or with my kids. For instance, if I married an Indian woman it would be easier to keep the Indian side of me alive. [That] kind of thing. So . . . depending on who I marry . . . how it's passed onto my kids, that will be a major [factor]. . . . In the ideal, I would like to learn Malayalam myself and pass it on. [It] won't happen . . . I mean, that's not going to happen. There's no way I'm going to learn Malayalam because it's really difficult to do that in the United States. [Prakash Moghadam]

> If I marry my boyfriend, who's black, and I live in a place that's predominantly black, and my children would obviously grow up being darker than I am . . . having two black parents. . . . Then, yeah, it would probably shift. [Donna Tesh]

Prakash and Donna, who generally identify as more Indian and black respectively, say the cultural influence of their future partners and surrounding community could (depending on their backgrounds) contribute to a deeper connection within a heritage group.

Four students say they are not sure why they suspect their ideas about their identities will change in the future. Kris says, "I'm sure they have [in the past]. I'm sure they're still changing. But from what to what, I'm not sure." Kay is very clear about why she feels her sense of ethnoracial identity will continue to develop, stating, "Oh yeah. It's been a big evolution and I would think that [my thoughts about my identity] would keep evolving. Especially like doing this research [project]." Based on her past experiences, Kay views the unfolding nature of her identity as an inherent part of her experience as a mixed heritage person. These types of com-

ments by the majority of mixed heritage students in this study suggest that they expect their experiences to fluctuate and would be
tolerant to changes in their ethnoracial self-concept.

Transmission of Identity

Another way the nature of ethnoracial identity among mixed
heritage students was explored was by considering their interpretations of their children's identities. The following question was
asked of students:

• How would you see your child's ethnoracial identity, and would it depend on anything?

Students clearly stated that it would depend on the ethnoracial
identity of their partner, or biological parent of the child. Several
students said they don't believe the other parent's background will
necessarily determine the child's identity, nor do they see the children as mere reproductions of their own backgrounds. Instead, they
would view their children's identities as a composite of both parents' ancestry, as Melanie and Prakash contend:

> It would depend on who I would marry. I would definitely
> want them to recognize everything that they are part of—
> what . . . they are. [Melanie Newheim]

> It depends on the background the woman's from. I mean, I
> would definitely emphasize that they were Indian in some
> respects. I would . . . want to keep my name, which of course
> would be under discussion with whoever I would be with.
> But I would emphasize that they were Indian. But if they
> were whatever else, I don't even know what the other per-
> son would be. [Prakash Moghadam]

> So if the person, for example, had a strong emphasis on their
> own ethnic heritage, would you foster that as well? [KW]

> Mmm hmm [yes]. [Prakash Moghadam]

Like Prakash, who describes wanting to pass on his Indian name,
most students mention specific ways they would raise their children to know about their background. Similar to Prakash, Kay and
Donna each emphasize the importance of having their children learn
about her heritage:

I like kids and I would like to have kids. But it's bizarre when I start thinking about who am I going to end up having kids with. What are they? They can end up being anything. Absolutely anything. . . . My Japanese culture means a lot for me . . . I'm sure they would get that from me. But . . . my sister [has] been going out with the same guy, who's Chicano, for . . . four . . . years. . . . It's kind of becoming a little more serious. . . . They might just end up getting married and having kids and stuff, and they're going to be Californian. . . . This is where California is going, I think. And thank God I live in California because that's where [notions] of race are breaking down a little bit more. . . . It would definitely depend on who [I marry]. [Kay Meki]

Oh definitely [it would depend]. Well obviously if I marry a black person, then they would definitely be black. If I marry a white person then I think it would be more of a question of reminding them that African American is part of their heritage. . . . Say if I . . . marry a white person and have a child and they don't have, like, particularly curly hair, or they don't have particularly African American features, then I'm not going to try force this identity of their being black if that's not what's going on for them. I would definitely remind them and encourage them to explore that part of their heritage, but I'm not going to force them. [Donna Tesh]

Some students with a recently European American heritage stress the importance of both the minority and majority heritage, as Sheila details:

It would depend on the father—what nationality the father was. If he was multiethnic, or if he was of one race, I'd [stress] both his race, or races, and mine to the child. I'd tell them the background, and we'd probably celebrate St. Patty's Day and a few other things. And we'd go out and educate the child about what their background [is], even if the kid's adopted. . . . Say the husband were Latino and I [am Irish and Chippewa], and the child were Asian, we'd celebrate all of the festivities . . . *Cinco de Mayo* and things like that. We'd educate the child . . . this is his background . . . this is . . . his culture, and educate the child about my two cultures. And then celebrate [the child's], depending on which specific country they were from. If they were from

Japan, we'd probably celebrate some of their festivals. They have a lot of festivals for the seasons. [Sheila Rafkin]

For majority–minority students, the importance of maintaining a connection with the minority community increases with the possibility of marrying beyond this community, while access to the white community is not normally seen as a problem.

The students' accounts imply an awareness of the role generational distance can play in the child's identity development. None of the students suggest their future children should identify with only one heritage and not another. Instead, most students say they prefer the idea of celebrating the child's diverse heritage, as well as their unique ethnoracial experience.

Confronting Bureaucracy: Race/Ethnicity Surveys

Contemporary race/ethnicity surveys facilitate the collection of data through the use of mutually exclusive categories of race and ethnicity. The less ambiguity, the easier it is collect, process, and analyze the data consistently across time, or so it is argued (Saluter 1992).

Students were asked the following probes in order to uncover their feelings about these surveys, how they respond when confronted with mutually exclusive categories, and what they think about the more open-ended survey format used to recruit subjects for this study:

- How do you feel if you have to check one box only?
- Does your response on these kinds of surveys ever change?
- What did you think about this survey versus other types of surveys? Why?

There was some variation among students' feelings in response to the first probe about having to identify using mutually exclusive categories. For different reasons, Kris, Donna, and Sandy say they aren't particularly bothered by having to "choose one box." Sandy was told early on by an elementary school teacher that she wasn't Asian, but white, because of the teacher's association of Asia with East Asia and her assumptions about Sandy's heritage:

Actually, when I was little . . . we'd take those standardized tests and I would always mark in "Asian" because Iran's in Asia. . . . Then one day the teacher came up to me and she was like, "You're not Asian, you're white." So I've been marking "white" ever since. . . . I was in third grade or fourth grade—I was like "Well no, I am." And she was all, "No, you're white." [Sandy Zubaida]

Sandy doesn't mind having to select only the white category because her appearance and experience in the mainstream white community make this a logical choice. Donna says she likes identifying as black, but does point out that she does like having the option of having her mixed heritage acknowledged because of the role it plays in her life. Finally, Kris explains why mutually exclusive categories do not bother her:

I don't really care what I am. I really don't think it matters. . . . I know that for some people it's really an issue—they think they have to choose or something. But for me, I don't care. . . . I generally do it for—like Stanford—saying I'm black would help me get in. I'd probably do it [on this survey] if I hadn't noticed the [mixed heritage section]. . . . If it doesn't really matter, then I'll check both black and white. And if there's a little blank, I'll put like half and half. . . . And [if] there's no way to do one and the other, then yeah, I usually choose black because I generally feel like society [sees me that way]. . . . It doesn't really bother me. [Kris Dawson]

Kris does not mind being limited to the black category because she realizes society sees her as black, and sometimes this works to her advantage. However, there is never a context when Kris would identify as solely white, preferring instead to identify as both black and white when there are not direct consequences for doing so.

Yvonne and Alex have mixed feelings about mutually exclusive categories and highlight both their positive and negative aspects. Alex says:

There's advantages and disadvantages. The advantage to having five boxes is one of 'em's going to be you. . . . Sometimes it's hard to even decipher . . . what you are or what you really want to put down as yourself. You know? Like, if you have five boxes, one says "African American," "Caucasian," and "Other." . . . If Other's not there, then I fill out "African American." . . . It's real hard to decipher what you are sometimes, 'cause things go so far back. . . . Sometimes it gets a little hectic and you just want to put "white" or "black." Make it very easy for yourself. . . . And then there's times when you want to be, "Yeah, I'm this and you're not. I'm an individual, I'm different." So there's advantages and disadvantages. [Alex Bell]

Both Yvonne and Alex feel mutually exclusive categories can help to alleviate some of the complexity of having to delineate exactly what they are on paper.

Ten of the fifteen students overwhelmingly agree that they do not like mutually exclusive categories. Several students noted that they make them uncomfortable because they are forced to choose one side of their heritage over the other, like Missy who contends, "That's kind of hard to do, it's . . . confusing." And Sheila's comments are especially poignant:

> I feel that [having to choose one category] eliminates the other half of me. . . . It makes me feel I'm being asked to cut off my other arm.·. . . Usually things don't bother me, but . . . think about it. There's half of me that's from North America, and there's another half of me that's from Europe. . . . Just . . . people always say to identify yourself . . . get to know yourself before you go on to other things. And they always talk about your self-confidence. But if you have to identify only half of yourself, then it's going against everything people have been talking about. [Sheila Rafkin]

Sheila eloquently states how being forced to select one heritage over another runs counter to all the lessons she has learned about developing her self-esteem and taking pride in her identity. Several students choose to subvert mutually exclusive categories when confronted with them:

> If [the form] had me . . . choose this or that . . . I would like cross those out and put what I am on there. [Steve Billings]

> It depends on the situation. . . . Sometimes I don't check a box. If I'm in that mind state, if I'm in the state "Why does it matter what race I am?" . . . Just recently we had a . . . Golden State Exam. . . . It said . . . it was optional, because they wanted to just separate groups. . . . And I was, like, "I'm not going to participate in that." . . . I didn't put nothing, you know? [Alex Bell]

> We take some of these at school . . . I don't usually fill them out . . . I think . . . it denies people who they really are. And

I'm not saying me, 'cause it's not that big of a deal for me as it is for other people. [But] it denies them where they're from. . . . But then sometimes I think it offends me. . . . It's just different every time. Sometimes I check both, sometimes I don't put anything. [Melanie Newheim]

As these comments reveal, these high school students feel traditional race/ethnicity surveys do not allow people to be accurately represented. Alex and Melanie also seem to think the surveys are divisive and serve no possible good. These students will sometimes transgress the boundaries that are imposed by mutually exclusive categories in order to provide a more ethical interpretation of their identities than is offered to them.

When asked what they thought about the open-ended format of the survey used to recruit the subjects for this study, two students were not too sure whether they liked it or not. Amanda, who tends to identify solely as a Christian, is the one student who believes moving away from mutually exclusive categories has potentially harmful consequences if the option is for mixed heritage people to be grouped together:

It's kind of problematic for me because . . . I just started check[ing] black [instead of "Other"]. And part of me, I don't know . . . it's hard to put into words. But I feel there is some sort of danger there for . . . mixed people to make themselves into one group because even within the mixed group there's all different kind of groups. And I think that standards that take away from the percentage of blacks living [in certain areas] is really dangerous. [Amanda Wilson]

Amanda's awareness of the broader sociopolitical consequences of race/ethnicity surveys influenced her to stop checking "other" and start marking "black." Again, Alex explains his concern about making surveys too complicated, "Your survey, I was like 'Whew! What am I really? Do I want to use that term or that term? Hmmm.' I was really stressing. I was like 'What do I want to put?'" Thirteen students say they liked the open-ended format of the survey for various reasons. Some prefer the available terminology (like the word "European American" in addition to "white"), while others appreciate the flexibility, as Karen and Marta contend:

It's hard when you . . . can only check one box. . . . That's why when I filled out yours . . . we could check as many boxes as [we wanted]. It was neat because I was able to

say I'm Native American, I'm Irish, I'm French and European. So it's not like it's narrowing myself to one thing. . . . I
didn't think anybody in this world is just one thing. . . .
Maybe the first person to create it was one thing, but then
people start mixing together. [Karen Loomis]

I really appreciate being able to check more than one thing.
Yeah. I always check Hispanic, but I feel uncomfortable
doing that. . . . Again, it goes back to what I was saying
before about how I feel like I don't want to cut off that side
of me, either. . . . There's a lot of assumptions that people
make based on looking at your name on a piece of paper. .
. . And I don't like the word Hispanic . . . but I check it
because that's usually what's available. [Marta Elizondo]

While Karen is fourth generation biracial/ethnic, and Marta generally identifies as Mexican American, both emphasize how they
dislike traditional surveys because they gloss over the diversity of
people's identities.
   Many mixed heritage students have other opinions to share about
race/ethnicity surveys in general. Missy and Karen are the only
students who say they like these surveys; Missy says she finds them
"fun," and Karen enjoys having the opportunity to reveal to people
that she is of Native American Indian ancestry. Still, more students say they find surveys problematic. Donna, Prakash, and Kay
feel surveys, again, tend to oversimplify:

Race is a hard category. . . . We use race to decide things;
some of those things help and some of those things hurt. . . .
It's kind of a silly way to characterize people . . . maybe
just as silly as male/female. . . . People should be able to
put as many [as they want]. [Donna Tesh]

The problem with the census is where do you put people
then? . . . Race, . . . I generally don't think of it as a real
good way of classifying. I think ethnic classification is better . . . I would prefer that. [Prakash Moghadam]

When you're trying to do something like that I think you're
headed for [trouble]. . . . You can't capture . . . ethnicity or
what it means, or race and what that means. . . . Trying to
[make scientific] everything, trying to put everything into
a science. . . . Things . . . will be lost if you try and make an
Excel graph [of it]. . . . That's sort of a danger. [Kay Meki]

As a high school student, Alex wonders why data on race/ethnicity are needed sometimes:

> A lot of times I don't see why they need my race. Like, if I'm applying for college or something "Why you need my race?" I understand some colleges have quotas they have to fill. . . . But . . . I'm a high school [student]. . . . Like right now I get P.E. credits for basketball leagues that I attend at colleges, and they want to know my race . . . I just don't fill it out. Why does it matter? You know what I'm saying? I mean . . . I'm playing basketball just like this white dude's playing basketball, just like this Asian person's playing basketball, and just like . . . that purple dude is playing basketball. So it doesn't really matter. We're all basketball players. [Alex Bell]

As these comments reveal, some students understand that there are political and legal needs for collecting data by race/ethnicity, while others view the forms as largely unnecessary. Finally, many of the mixed heritage students interviewed here feel mutually exclusive categories, and specifically racial categories, are inadequate vehicles for describing their identities.

On Being "Both/And"

Several probes attempted to target what "being" a certain ethnicity/race means for mixed heritage students. In general, students of latter-generation European heritage had difficulty defining whiteness or white ethnic identity unless it was juxtaposed to their minority ancestry. Those of more recent European ethnic ancestry were able to articulate more clearly the nature of group membership.

Sheila has very concrete ideas about what being both Native American Indian and Irish American mean:

> It explains some of the traits I have. It explains why I prefer . . . to recycle. . . . And it explains why sometimes I get blood-boiling angry. It explains some of my physical traits. It explains some of my love for Europe and my love to stay on native soil, so to speak. I don't know. If I ever get the chance to go out to see Ireland and Minnesota, I'll probably be able to answer that question a lot better. [Sheila Rafkin]

Sheila attributes certain values, behaviors, and physical traits to the influence of her dual ancestry. Melanie, who is second generation

biracial, says she is not sure what being both European and Mexican American means: "I don't know much about it. That's why I
was kind of doubting if [I should be in this study]. . . . I'm not half
something and half-another, [and I told my mom] 'I don't think
that's good enough for her' [Melanie Newheim]."

Being one-quarter Latino, Melanie was concerned because she is
one generation removed from an immediately mixed experience,
which suggests that terms such as "mixed" and "biracial/ethnic"
(like traditional categories of ethnicity and race) have the propen-
sity to reify certain experiences and marginalize others.

Several students say feelings of marginalization and illegitimacy
are part and parcel of a mixed heritage experience. Marta clarifies
how her mixed heritage affects her sense of being Mexican American:

> Part of what's hard about being mixed . . . [is that] biologi-
> cally I'm not really Mexican. But if you look at some of the
> traditions and some of the things in how I grew up, [they're]
> very much Mexican American. . . . And it gets hard when
> people start telling you "Well you're not, because this, that,
> and whatever." . . . What else do I have to do, what quali-
> fies me? [Marta Elizondo]

Marta describes her mixed parentage as diluting her sense of cultural legitimacy in the Mexican American community, even though
her ethnic experience is very much grounded in the group. Prakash
also wonders about his membership status and says simply, "There
are questions of where do I fit in, [that] kind of thing." Again, Alex
spells the pluses and minuses to being both black and white:

> Sometimes my mom . . . she'll ask me, "Does it bother you
> that you're part white?" 'Cause, you know, [my parents
> are] divorced. And I'll be, "Not really." 'Cause it has its
> advantages—being mixed—and has its disadvantages at
> the same time. I mean, as far as that goes, no. It hasn't
> really come up as a big deal since my childhood. Since when
> they used to call [me] Oreo and stuff. [Alex Bell]

Alex refers to being teased by peers as one of the disadvantages of
having mixed heritage. Kris feels that being black and white does
and does not affect her at the same time:

> I guess that I don't know if my [ethnic] identity . . . has
> that much to do with my racial identity. . . . Generally,
> when I'm just thinking of myself and what it means to me,

it's not really an issue. Because I think it's really an outward thing [about] what people expect. . . . It really affects
me in terms of society . . . not really in seeing myself . . . as
a representative of [a certain group]. . . . I think that's a lot
of the reason why labels don't really matter that much,
because it's not reflected on me, my inner person. It's just
a way to classify people. [Kris Dawson]

Kris emphasizes the difference between how she feels and how society sees her; she explains that there is a mismatch between the
labels that are applied to her and how she actually feels, which is
more ethnically white.

Marta and Amanda both mention how being biracial/ethnic has
meaning through their family experiences and relationships with
individual family members. Amanda says being both Jamaican
American and Chinese American means being a part of both of her
parents, while Marta references her extended family:

[Being both] means having two sets of cousins. I have one
set of cousins that are all fair hair . . . light eyes, and light
skin. And we're right smack dab in the middle . . . and the
language thing. Not having the dialect of a lot of my cousins who are Mexican . . . who didn't have mixed parents
[and] have the Chicano dialect and/or speak Spanish. . . . I
think another thing is that—I don't know why—[but] on
both sides of my family, I'm the first one who went to college. And I don't understand why. I kind of understand
from my Mexican side . . . because traditionally Mexicans
are not expected to go and [so on]. But on my other side of
the family, I don't know why that's true. . . . I don't know
why it would be [that with] the combination of the two
families, I think ours had been the most successful in terms
of education. [Marta Elizondo]

Steve and Jocelyn relate being biracial/ethnic to finding a home in
more than one group, while Jocelyn claims being first generation
Swiss and Indian is a rich experience:

It just means I have so much to draw from. I can go lots of
different places and feel [welcomed]. . . . I feel more welcome in India than I did in Switzerland, only because [there
it's like] "How can you be Swiss because of the way that
you look?" And that hurts. So I don't feel as comfortable
there. . . . It just means that I can draw on a lot of different

kinds of experiences and values and tradition. [Jocelyn Saghal]

While the reception may be different, Jocelyn still finds a sense of home and identity in both heritage communities.

But Yvonne and Kay feel that there is a solitary dimension to a mixed heritage existence. Yvonne discusses how being from a mixed background can be very isolating:

> People of mixed backgrounds . . . [there are] a lot of things that you go through [which] you think [are] unique to you . . . and nobody else feels. . . . But . . . just reading through the literature [helps]. . . . When I did . . . my freshman English paper I picked biracial kids [as a topic]. . . . And, so, you have to go look in psych[ology] . . . to find these three articles. . . . But the ones I did find . . . were pretty good. I felt . . . that they explained different types of mixed race kids. . . . And I think every mix is going to be unique. . . . But . . . I think . . . that helped me a lot to understand . . . things that I had gone through. . . . It helped me be more comfortable with my identity. Whereas, before I was . . . just not sure of what I was or what. [Yvonne Garcia]

Yvonne's comments show how learning about other mixed heritage people's experiences helped to make her feel less isolated and more comfortable with her identity when she was in college. Kay also speaks about how being both Japanese American–European American contributes to her sense of solitude:

> I think . . . if I'm in a totally safe space that's what I am [both Japanese–European American]. But when I'm sort of out there, with people who I know don't understand— don't understand what it means to be mixed race—I don't have the luxury of really fully being that. That's why it's so hard for me to sort of be mixed all the time, because there's no context for me, there's no context. . . . When I went to Japan there was no context there, either. . . . So I think that's why it's really exciting that you're doing this research. . . . I would hope that [it] . . . would . . . make it easier for me to . . . talk about it freely with everyone else. . . . Not just when I'm with people who are also mixed. . . . It would just . . . be understood. It would be more a general topic, it's more accepted. [Kay Meki]

Kay concisely articulates how there is no space for realizing a mixed heritage identity in the United States. Because there is no public awareness about "what it means to be mixed race," Kay adjusts her identity accordingly when interacting with others. Only on occasion, in a community of other mixed heritage individuals, can Kay be afforded the "luxury of really being fully" both Japanese and European American.

Like Kay, a few of the students remark how opportunities for expressing their mixed identities are few and far between. As Alex and Jocelyn note, these opportunities opened up while at school:

> My English teacher [talked about being mixed] this year. But that's because her parents were mixed, and she was adopted so she doesn't know exactly what she is. . . . Her dad was Caribbean and her mother was Spanish or something. So she basically just wanted to know where I was coming from. The same with [another teacher]. That's about it. [Alex Bell]

> I don't think the discussion occurs really. . . . I remember once we had a word in vocabulary . . . I think it was . . . Eurasian. . . . I was a junior in high school and my friend was like, "Oh, you're Eurasian." And I remember there was a full discussion. She went to the teacher and [asked] "Well, is Jocelyn Eurasian?" . . . Then the teacher said, "Well, [if she's] from Europe . . . and [if she's] from Asia." . . . There was a little discussion about that. It was kind of interesting. I think it might have been the first time [encountering the word]. I would just say I was mixed. I never really had any other kind of vocabulary for it, I don't think. . . . Except for "other." [Jocelyn Saghal]

These comments and the lack of similar experiences among the other students suggest that a mixed heritage orientation is not recognized as a possible and positive identity orientation.

Finally, Donna sees another way of framing what other mixed heritage students generally view as a solitary experience: "Interracial relationships [and] marriage—it feels like being on the cutting edge. . . . Always like the flavor of the month . . . I don't know. I think it's cool to be [biracial/ethnic]" [Donna Tesh].

As topics related to interracial/ethnic relationships and mixed heritage people are emerging in the media with greater frequency, Donna sees being mixed as a new trend. Perhaps this means that some individuals of mixed heritage will come to recognize their common experiences as greater attention is paid to them in the mass media.

SUMMARY

In this chapter, I explore what being mixed, or of multiple heritage means for these fifteen students and consider where their experiences converge. The students have many different interpretations of their mixed heritage, but find themselves on common ground in many ways.

Occupying a unique ethnic and racial status based on their ancestry and often complex cultural experiences, these students describe occupying a unique position in U.S. society. On the one hand, their status leads to marginalization within their heritage communities, minority and dominant alike. Not having a choice in how or where they were raised, students speak about feeling pressured to prove their cultural legitimacy or even change how they identify, reinforcing their perceptions of being in the borderlands between communities and not quite a full member of either group. On the other hand, the experience of being doubly-marginalized lends itself to an egalitarian outlook in the ways these students identify themselves, refusing to deny or privilege one heritage community over the other. Even for those students whose ethnic experiences are grounded in a mainstream community, as adults many seek to establish a greater balance in their experience by learning more about a group's history and culture, as well as developing meaningful relationships with group members. Their flexible orientations toward their mixed heritage reflect their dynamic and diverse experiences at the interface of race and culture.

NOTE

1. This suggests that students' experiences attending a predominantly white college may impact their sense of proximity to their minority community of heritage. However, most of the university students say they were raised in predominantly white settings as well, unlike the high school students in this study.

Chapter 7

Conclusions and Educational Implications

This study explores the processes involved in the development of ethnic and racial identity for students of recently mixed heritage. The previous chapters investigate the factors at play in the construction of these identities across social and temporal contexts. This chapter provides an overview of the study's findings, as well as their implications for educational practice and policy.

ETHNIC AND RACIAL IDENTITY DEVELOPMENT

Origins and Issues

The roots of ethnic identity among these fifteen students are complex, as would be expected among individuals of recently mixed heritage. Within the home, the parents' orientations toward their own ethnic identity have a powerful influence on the meaning mixed heritage students confer upon ethnic group membership. Among latter generation, multiethnic European American parents, ethnic identity is seen as optional and plays a largely symbolic role in their lives. By contrast, ethnic identity is seen as relevant in the daily lives of parents who are racialized minorities or whose families immigrated to the United States in the past three generations. Within each family unit, then, mixed heritage students can be exposed to differing community approaches toward ethnic identity.

In this way, interracial/ethnic families are a microcosm of ethnic life in the United States.

As a whole, these students have diverse experiences with respect to their heritage communities, from almost exclusive participation within one to extensive participation within both. The relative depth of participation within a community has a direct impact on mixed heritage students' ethnic identity development since ongoing interaction within a heritage community creates opportunities for acquiring its Discourse. The home alone does afford meaningful opportunities for acquiring a Discourse, but they are deepened when a Discourse reaches beyond the family and into the local community. Only a few students in this study describe relatively sustained participation within both heritage communities over the course of their childhood and adolescence. Due to factors beyond their control, several of the students lacked access to one heritage community beyond their relationship with a parent or relative. For many, local population ratios afforded deep participation in one community and more limited participation in the other. And it is important to note that for a number of students, their degree of participation in a heritage community shifted over the course of their lives as their families moved.

Physical appearance is also important to the ethnic identity development process of mixed heritage students. In a racially ordered society, physical features are often linked to ethnic group membership. Almost all the students have been asked to clarify their racial ambiguity, reinforcing the role physical appearance plays within the maintenance of the racial order. Most of these students describe how their physical appearance precludes or complicates the degree to which community members accept, or even recognize them as a part of the group regardless of their ethnic heritage or cultural upbringing. While this may be expected within the mainstream European American community with its strict standards of whiteness, it is also the case within racialized minority communities. Despite the fact that many racialized minority groups are more flexible in their tolerance of internal physical diversity, most students find their appearance is a roadblock to recognition and acceptance within these communities. The degree to which physical appearance is a more substantial or less significant barrier depends on other factors as well, most notably whether the individual is well apprenticed in the community's Discourse. Variations within the community encourage the reinforcement of group boundaries through the marginalization of those who represent difference (e.g., the mixed heritage person learning the community Discourse as a college student) until they can sufficiently demonstrate their proficiency in the Discourse, thereby ensuring its continuation.

Like ethnic identity, lessons about racial identity are also subtly transmitted within the home. Only a couple of students received overt messages from their parents about their mixed racial heritage. It is through their interactions with peers within the heritage communities, in particular, that these students learn the most about their relative status within a group as people of mixed racial ancestry. As mentioned, the credential of one's heritage is not necessarily grounds for full citizenship within a racial community. The first generation students note how physical appearance, Discourse style, and the fact of their mixed heritage contribute to their relatively liminal status in both heritage groups.

These mixed heritage students see themselves as having qualitatively different experiences from their single heritage peers in several ways. Growing up in an interracial, interethnic family structure and having recently mixed heritage provide an important context that shapes their ethnoracial identity development. Also important to the process is navigating between cultural contexts, reflecting on the different standards of each context, and the experience of marginalization within a heritage community. And finally, having to explain their heritage either to satisfy someone's curiosity or to prove group membership is another way mixed heritage students learn that their unique background plays a role in how they are seen by their heritage communities.

Approaches

The mixed heritage students in this study identify with their respective communities in myriad ways. The thirteen part-white students are not able to describe in detail what it feels like to be ethnically European American, and describe the experience instead as one that is a racialized and postethnic. By contrast, most students are able to describe how it feels to be a part of their minority heritage group by bringing out specific cultural elements to characterize the experience. Interestingly, many of these students do point to the cultural dimensions of being white but do not have a framework for interpreting it in ethnic terms. For example, they may talk about the culture (worldviews, attitudes, behaviors, etc.) of their white relatives or mainstream community in general as distinct from the experiences of a particular racialized minority community. This suggests that many students' experiences in the mainstream (or other white communities) juxtaposed to their experiences in racialized minority communities, help to make visible the usually transparent culture of mainstream European American life.

Identity is dynamic among this group of mixed heritage students. Students tend to adjust both their behavior and ways of identifying across different social contexts depending on the nature of the interaction or situation. Although some students identify more strongly with one of their heritage communities, the most striking finding from the data is the existence of a stable, mixed heritage frame of reference. Using this frame of reference as a starting point, these students proceed to construct their ethnoracial identities in dynamic, often open-ended ways.

The universality of this mixed heritage frame of reference may be a reflection of some common experiences among these students. For many, their experiences at the interface of cultures place them at an unusual vantage point for thinking about intergroup relations and tolerating difference. And all students were born and raised at a time in U.S. history when diversity has been greatly emphasized. The acknowledgment of their mixed heritage ultimately may be a way for these students to honor the diversity and pluralism that their families embody, while allowing for flexibility in how they identify in terms of ethnicity and race.

EDUCATIONAL IMPLICATIONS

By unraveling some of the dimensions of ethnic and racial identity development among mixed heritage students in the prior chapters, my intent was threefold. First, I hoped to make explicit how ethnic and racial identities come into existence through social interaction. Second, I wished to detail how mixed heritage students make sense of these constructions. And finally, I wanted to show how these processes are imbedded in the social relations of schools.

Students, teachers, administrators, and staff bring to bear a wealth of knowledge in their interactions at school. The transmission of cultural knowledge does not stop at the front door; schools are places where social identities are produced, reproduced, and contested through people's relationships with one another and the school curriculum. Kids spend a great deal of their time in schools, making them critical spaces where they assert, question, test, and reinvent their identities through their interactions with their peers. Educators concerned with fostering a supportive environment for mixed heritage students must address the nature of the social relationships and the curriculum at their schools.

Peer relationships are principal sites where conflicts around ethnic and racial identity are acted out. Recognizing how inter- and intragroup conflict has the potential to affect mixed heritage children should be of particular concern for counselors, teachers, and administrators. Like any student, those of mixed heritage may experience having one or both heritage groups demeaned by their peers. Mixed heritage students may also find themselves caught in the middle of intergroup tensions and asked to choose sides by defending a heritage community at the expense of the other. It is imperative for adults to recognize how the mixed heritage student, in particular, is affected by such a call to deny, disparage, or defend one community over the other. Intragroup testing is another source of pressure at school as mixed heritage students are marginalized by community members because of how they look, act, or talk. Finally, being of recently mixed heritage may also be stigmatized, although this will vary by region and community. Whether it is due to intragroup or intergroup conflict, mixed heritage students are at risk of having their ancestry or aspects of their heritage disparaged in ways that are qualitatively different from their same-heritage peers.

Teachers and other school staff need professional development opportunities to explore their attitudes and exposure to stereotypes about intermarriage and mixed heritage children. Different groups have different attitudes about exogamy and about the identity of children born to interracial/ethnic couples. Educators need to examine their personal biases to determine how they may inadvertently preference or penalize mixed heritage students. Ideas of the mixed person as a "model" minority or a "confused" individual are just some of the common stereotypes that continue to be seen in the media and in literature.

One of the important findings from this project is how mixed heritage students see their experiences as largely invisible and solitary. While the high school students in this study were raised in a region where there is a much higher concentration of interracial/ethnic families, their relatively small numbers in the United States in general mean that many will grow up in isolation from peers of similarly mixed ancestry. Students infrequently had opportunities to discuss their experiences and issues; when they did, they occurred mostly through conversations with siblings. These demographic realities, coupled with the relative invisibility of interracial/ethnic families in the society at large, contribute to a sense of solitude and uniqueness for many mixed heritage students. And like other minority students in mainstream settings, these mixed heritage students resent being referred to as an ethnic "expert" by teachers. Labeling anyone an ethnic expert by virtue of their heritage is unfair, but it may be especially complicated for mixed heritage students who often feel that their dual ancestry does not entitle them to speak for the community.

Several steps can be taken to alter the school curriculum in recognition of students who come from mixed heritage backgrounds. Within the formal curriculum, it is important to examine how human diversity is portrayed through representations of culture and race, especially in the overt teaching of these concepts. Mixed heritage experiences should be woven into a school's general and multicultural curricular efforts in a way that does not segregate the content. Within the curriculum, identifying with one's mixed heritage should be presented as a viable, legitimate alternative for some individuals. This recognition of a mixed heritage alternatives must be tempered with the understanding that not all mixed individuals identify the same way, nor should they be expected to. Providing students with choices in how they identify (as Japanese American, as African American, or as both) will foster a more tolerant, supportive environment. Librarians and teachers, in particular, can help to make their experiences more visible by expanding the curriculum to include literature with mixed heritage themes and opportunities for students to express their personal lives in ways that do not spotlight them as exotic or unusual. Including a multiracial/ethnic perspective in the school setting needs to be realized naturally without overemphasizing this difference, which may further create a feeling of being isolated.

Schools should examine their use of surveys for bias and begin to formulate alternative strategies for collecting data by race and ethnicity.[1] This is important to consider in light of the proliferation of high-stakes standardized tests, which may ask students to identify themselves in mutually exclusive terms before they take the test. Several states and school systems around the country have already begun to change how they gather and report such data. In sum, educators must think about the types of messages they are conveying about race, culture, and mixed heritage both inside and outside of the classroom. The approach a school takes toward addressing human diversity ultimately impacts every member of the educational community.

William Pinar notes that "curriculum debates about what we teach the young are . . . debates about who we perceive ourselves to be and how we will represent that identity, including what remains 'left over,' as 'difference'" (Pinar and Reynolds 1992). The advent of multicultural education has contributed enormously to more positive intergroup relations and greater knowledge about the cultural discontinuities that may exist between the school and home. One of the many limitations of multiculturalism in education has been to reify a modernist framework of human identity that denies the existence of mixed heritage people. I hope these students' stories will urge educators to rethink this framework and begin to work more critically on diversity issues in their schools.

CONCLUSION

The past decade has brought to our attention the interracial/ethnic realities of U.S. society. Through magazines, popular literature, and the recent television talk show craze, mixed heritage topics are finding their way into the public's eye with increasing frequency. As more interracial/ethnic couples join together and have mixed heritage children, even the Office of Management and Budget has been forced to change how data are collected by categories of race and ethnicity (Tucker and Kojetin 1996).

The mixed heritage students in this study were raised in a social climate marked by a resurgence of racial pride, equal rights movements, and a budding multiculturalism. While the legacy of popular multiculturalism is at best benign and at worst oppressive in its consequences, its egalitarian framework nonetheless is one of its most enduring and influential features, as made evident through students' stories. The value these students place on their heritage and diverse experiences suggest that there is a strong desire to present more fluid, complex expressions of identity in today's multicultural United States. Mixed heritage students are finding ways to resist traditional identity discourses by crafting new ways and spaces in which to challenge them.

I realize that by suggesting our traditional models of race are becoming increasingly inefficient in describing our social world could be interpreted by some people that race has lost its salience in U.S. life. Scholarship such as this might be seen as evidence for those who want to do away, at least superficially, with all things racial in the name of a society that is racially neutral and legally color-blind. In an era where regressive political movements are undermining the precious gains made in recent decades, I also recognize how this work may be seen as potential ammunition aimed at the health and well-being of racialized minority communities. Nonetheless, the ultimate intention of this research is to illuminate the enduring and changing face of race at this particular point in U.S. history. Race is an inextricable part of our identity as a society, and life at the interface between races is a critical site for learning more about it.

NOTE

1. The use of mutually exclusive categories of race/ethnicity will eventually be phased out as the new categories approved by the OMB take effect after the 2000 census.

Appendix A

Race–Ethnicity Survey

Name: _____   Age: _____

Place of Birth: _____   Sex: male/female
              city and state or country   please circle one

Year: _____

Grade/Major: _____

Primary Language(s): _____

Please check as many of the subcategories within as many of the groups you feel best describe your ethnic and racial heritage. If something is not included, please write it in on the lines provided for "other group/word."

Asian or Pacific Islander American, etc.

Please check as many as apply:

( ) Asian–Asian American   ( ) Japanese
( ) Asian Indian   ( ) Korean
( ) Cambodian   ( ) Laotian
( ) Chinese   ( ) Micronesian

( ) Fijian   ( ) Pacific Islander
( ) Filipino   ( ) Tongan
( ) Hawaiian   ( ) Vietnamese
( ) Hmong
( ) Other group/word:
                                          _____
                                          Please describe above
( ) Other group/word:
                                          _____
                                          Please describe above

Black/African American, etc.

Please check as many as apply:

( ) African American   ( ) Central, South American
( ) Black   ( ) North African
( ) Caribbean   ( ) Puerto Rican
( ) Cuban   ( ) Sub-Saharan African
( ) Other group/word:
                                          _____
                                          Please describe above
( ) Other group/word:
                                          _____
                                          Please describe above

Latino-a or Hispanic American, etc.

Please check as many as apply:

( ) Central, South American   ( ) Latino-a
( ) Cuban   ( ) Mexican American/Chicano-a
( ) Hispanic   ( ) Puerto Rican
( ) Other group/word:
                                          _____
                                          Please describe above
( ) Other group/word:
                                          _____
                                          Please describe above

Native–Indigenous American, etc.

Please check as many as apply:

( ) Aleut   ( ) Native American
( ) Eskimo   ( ) Native Hawaiian
( ) Indian   ( ) Native Samoan, Guamanian,
( ) Native Alaskan   or other Native Pacific Islander
( ) Other group/word:
                                          _____
                                          Please describe above

( ) Other group/word: _____
                        Please describe above

White/European American, etc.

Please check as many as apply:

( ) Caucasian   ( ) North African
( ) English   ( ) Portuguese
( ) European American   ( ) Scottish
( ) Irish   ( ) Spanish
( ) Middle Eastern   ( ) White
( ) Other group/word: _____
                          Please describe above
( ) Other group/word: _____
                          Please describe above

Recent Biracial or Multiracial Heritage*

*Biracial and multiracial heritage here refers to having parents or grandparents of birth who are considered to be from two or more different racial backgrounds.

( ) Biracial Heritage (Please indicate your racial heritage below)

        mother's heritage: _____

        father's heritage: _____

( ) Multiracial Heritage (Please indicate your racial heritage below)

        mother's heritage: _____

        father's heritage: _____

( ) Other word: _____
(e.g., mixed, mixed race, mulatto-a, hapa, métis, Amerasian, etc.)

Appendix B

===

Recruitment Flyer

[name of student]

_____, I would really like to talk with you!

I'm doing research on individuals like myself, of mixed/biracial heritage, and I'm contacting you to see if you'd be willing to participate in my study.

I'd like to interview you to learn more about your experiences growing up and in school, regardless of how you identify yourself.

The interviews won't take much of your time—anywhere from 1–5 hours. All information will be kept confidential—no names will be used.

Please read the attached information and return the consent form to your teacher, noting if you are or are not interested in participating. Also, if you are eighteen or older you do not need your parents'/guardians' consent to participate.

Appendix C

Expressive Autobiographical Interview Probes

Tell me about yourself and your family.

> When and where were you born and raised?
>
> Where were your parents from? How did they meet?
>
> Mother's/father's occupation? Occupations since your birth?
>
> What is/was your family like? (relationships with brothers, sisters, cousins, other relatives, etc.)
>
> What does your family like to do together? (religious, social, casual, formal, professional, etc.)

Do you think you are a lot, a little, or not at all like your mother?

> If yes, how? If no, why not?
>
> Look alike? (features, color)
>
> Act alike? (clothing, speech/language, mannerisms, etc.)
>
> Alike in other ways? (religion, beliefs, interests, etc.)
>
> Have you had people tell you how alike or different you are from her? (give example)

Do you think you are a lot, a little, or not at all like your father?

> If yes, how? If no, why not?
>
> Look alike? (features and color)

Act alike? (clothing, speech/language, mannerisms, etc.)

Alike in other ways? (religion, beliefs, interests, etc.)

Have you had people tell you how alike or different you are from him? (give example)

When in public with your mother, father, or siblings, how do strangers interact with you?

Do they assume that you are related?

Have you ever had someone assume that you were not together?

Growing up, did your parent/s talk about their own ethnic, racial heritage, or identity?

If yes, can you think of a time recently? (give example)

If no, why do you think it wasn't talked about?

Growing up, did anyone in your family talk about your own ethnic, racial heritage, or identity?

If yes, can you think of a time recently? (give example)

If no, why do you think it wasn't talked about?

Have you and your sibling(s) ever talked about being (member of X group) and (member of Y group)?

Growing up, how did your parent(s) talk about people being different?

What kinds of things did they say about interracial couples, about your ethnicity, about mixed heritage children, etc.?

Can you look back and see any general messages that they gave you?

Have you gone through times in your life when you have been told that you had to choose to be one or another race?

If yes, tell me about these times. What led up to this? What happened? Why do you think it mattered?

Tell me about your life at school (K–12 experiences).

Favorite or least favorite classes and why?

Any classes you like but cannot take? If yes, why?

What are your close friends like (common interests)? Do they like school?

Are you a part of any school organizations or teams (K–12)?

What do you like most or like least about being in school right now and why?

Do your parents help you with your school work?

Do you know how your parents felt about going to school?

Did your parents go to college? If yes, how many years did they complete?

Has there ever been a time at school when your mixed heritage mattered or came up? (e.g., in class, an assignment, teacher comment, clubs, friends, etc.)

If yes, tell me about this. What led up to this? What happened? Why do you think it mattered?

Tell me about your life outside of high school.

Who are your close friends? What do you like to do together? Why do you think you are friends with them? (give example)

What types of things do you like to do? (give example)

Any job or work related activities? (give example)

Do you participate in any informal or organized groups or activities? (give example)

Do you have any dating experiences and any preferences? (give example)

Have you noticed that there are times you change the way you talk depending on the context you are in? If yes, please describe.

What do you think about school?

Do you think you are a good student?

What do you think you will do after you graduate? (If not going to college)

Do you see yourself going to college? If no, why not?

Do you and your parents talk about your going to college?

Do your friends talk about going to college?

Have you ever had someone you do not know or do not know well ask you about your ethnic or racial heritage and/or identity? Has this ever happened at school?

If yes, what led up to this? What happened? Why do you think it mattered?

Have you ever had someone give you a hard time about your mixed heritage? Has this ever happened at school?

If yes, what led up to this? What happened? Why do you think it mattered?

How did you feel about it?

Did teachers or counselors do anything?

With respect to how you responded on the race/ethnicity survey you filled out:

What did you think about the survey versus other types of surveys? Why?

How do you feel if you have to check one box only?

Does your response on these kinds of surveys ever change?

Do you know how the government or your school classifies your racial heritage? That of your sibling(s)?

How do you see yourself today if you had to identify racially/ethnically?

Are there any particular words that you like to use to describe your ethnic, racial heritage, or identity?

Why do you think you identify this way?

Does this change depending on the person with whom you are talking?

How do you think others (family, siblings, teachers, friends, strangers) see you and why? Perhaps due to:

physical appearance (features, color, hair, etc.)

language or dialect or both

name

other (clothing, speech, mannerisms, etc.)

Is language somehow important in the [X] community? In the [Y] community? If so, how and why, in your opinion?

Do you ever feel more, or see yourself as more [X] sometimes? Can you give me an example?

Are there times when you feel more [Y]? Can you give me an example?

Would there ever be a time when you would identify solely as [X]? Can you give me an example?

Would there ever be a time when you would identify solely as [Y]? Can you give me an example?

Have you ever had strangers or people you don't know well make comments about how you look, positive and/or negative?

> If yes, tell me about these times. What led up to this? What happened? What types of things were said? Why do you think it mattered to them?

Have your parents or friends ever encouraged you to try to change your physical appearance?

> If yes, tell me about these times. What led up to this? What happened? Why do you think it mattered to them?

Do you think your ideas about your racial or ethnic identity have changed?

> If yes, how and why?
> Do you think they will change in the future? Why or why not?

Have you ever wanted to identify with all parts of your ethnic or racial heritage and not been able to?

> If yes, tell me about these times. What led up to this? What happened? Why do you think that it mattered?

What does "being" [X] mean for you and why?

What does "being" [Y] mean for you and why?

What does being both [X] and [Y] mean for you and why?

Do you think people with parents from the same racial background go through what you have gone through growing up? Why or why not?

If you have children someday, how would you view their ethnic/racial identity? Would it depend on anything in particular?

References

Anthias, F., and N. Yuval-Davis. 1992. *Racialized Boundaries: Race, Nation, Gender, Colour and Class and the Anti-Racist Struggle*. London: Routledge.

Anzaldúa, G. 1987. *Borderlands/La Frontera: The New Mestiza*. San Francisco: Aunt Lute Books.

Azoulay, K. G. 1997. *Black, Jewish and Interracial: It's Not the Color of Your Skin, but the Race of Your Kin*. Durham, N.C.: Duke University Press.

Bhabha, H. 1990. The Third Space: Interview with Homi Bhabha. In J. Rutherford (ed.), *Identity: Community, Culture, Difference*. London: Lawrence and Wishart.

Borman, K., and M. Y. Baber. 1998. *Ethnic Diversity in Communities and Schools: Recognizing and Building on Strengths*. Stamford, Conn.: Ablex.

Bradshaw, C. K. 1992. Beauty and the Beast: On Racial Ambiguity. In M.P.P. Root (ed.), *Racially Mixed People in America*. Newbury Park, Calif.: Sage Publications.

Brandt, G. L. 1994. *The Realization of Anti-Racist Teaching*. London: Falmer Press.

Burkey, R. M. 1978. *Ethnic and Racial Groups: The Dynamics of Dominance*. Menlo Park, Calif.: Cummings.

Carey, N., and E. Farris. 1996. *Racial and Ethnic Classifications Used by Public Schools*. Washington, D.C.: U.S. Department of Education, National Center for Education Statistics.

Castanell, L. A., and W. F. Pinar, eds. 1993. *Understanding Curriculum as Racial Text*. Albany: State University of New York Press.

Cauce, A. M., Y. Hiraga, C. Mason, T, Aguilar, N. Ordonez, and N. Gonzalez. 1992. Between a Rock and a Hard Place: Social Adjustment of Biracial Youth. In M.P.P. Root (ed.), *Racially Mixed People in America*. Newbury Park, Calif.: Sage Publications.

Cotter, J. S. 1990. *The Complete Poems of Joseph Seamon Cotter, Jr.* Edited by J. R. Payne. Athens: University of Georgia Press.

Cross, W. E., Jr. 1991. *Shades of Black: Diversity in African American Identity*. Philadelphia: Temple University Press.

Cross, W. E., Jr., and P. Fhagen-Smith. 1996. Nigrescence and Ego Identity Development: Accounting for Differential Black Identity Patterns. In P. Perdersen, J. Draguns, W. Lonner, and J. Trimble (eds.), *Counseling across Cultures*. Thousand Oaks, Calif.: Sage Publications.

Daniel, G. R. 1996. Black and White Identity in the New Millennium: Unsevering the Ties That Bind. In M.P.P. Root (ed.), *The Multiracial Experience: Racial Borders as the New Frontier*. Newbury Park, Calif.: Sage Publications.

————. 1992. Beyond Black and White: The New Multiracial Consciousness. In M.P.P. Root (ed.), *Racially Mixed People in America*. Newbury Park, Calif.: Sage Publications.

Davidson, A. L. 1992. *The Politics and Aesthetics of Ethnicity: Making and Molding Identity in Varied Curricular Settings*. Ph.D. diss., Stanford University.

Davis, F. J. 1991. *Who Is Black? One Nation's Definition*. University Park: Pennsylvania State University Press.

Denzin, N. K. 1992. *Symbolic Interaction and Cultural Studies: The Politics of Interpretation*. Oxford: Blackwell.

Ehrlich, P. R., and S. S. Feldman. 1977. *The Race Bomb: Skin Color, Prejudice, and Intelligence*. New York: Quadrangle/New York Times Book Co.

Erickson, E. H. 1963. *Childhood and Society*. 2d ed. New York: W. W. Norton.

Erickson, F. 1987. Transformation and School Success: The Politics and Culture of Educational Achievement. *Anthropology and Education Quarterly* 18 (4): 335–355.

Fernández, C. 1992. La Raza and the Melting Pot: A Comparative Look at Multiethnicity. In M.P.P. Root (ed.), *Racially Mixed People in America*. Newbury Park, Calif.: Sage Publications.

Fordham, S., and J. U. Ogbu. 1986. Black Students' School Success: Coping with the "Burden of Acting White." *Urban Review* 18 (3): 176–206.

Garfinkle, H. 1967. *Studies in Ethnomethodology*. Englewood Cliffs, N.J.: Prentice Hall.

Gay, G. 1997. Educational Equality for Students of Color. In J. Banks and C. M. Banks (eds.), *Multicultural Education: Issues and Perspectives*. Needham Heights, Mass.: Allyn and Bacon.

Gee, J. P. 1992. Society. In *The Social Mind: Language, Ideology and Social Practice*. New York: Bergin & Garvey.

————. 1990. *Social Linguistics and Literacies: Ideology in Discourses*. London: Falmer Press.

Gibbs, J. T., and A. M. Hines. 1992. Identity Development in Biracial Children. In M.P.P. Root (ed.), *Racially Mixed People in America*. Newbury Park, Calif.: Sage Publications.

Giroux, H. 1992. *Border Crossings: Cultural Workers and the Politics of Education*. New York: Routledge.

Giroux, H., ed. 1991. *Post-Modernism, Feminism, and Cultural Politics: Redrawing Educational Boundaries*. Albany: State University of New York Press.

Glass, R., and K. R. Wallace. 1996. Challenging Race and Racism: A Framework for Educators. In M.P.P. Root (ed.), *The Multiracial Experience: Racial Borders as the New Frontier*. Newbury Park, Calif.: Sage Publications.

Graham, S. 1996. The Real World. In M.P.P. Root (ed.), *The Multiracial Experience: Racial Borders as the New Frontier*. Newbury Park, Calif.: Sage Publications.

Grumet, M. 1993. Preface. In L. A. Castanell and W. F. Pinar (eds.), *Understanding Curriculum as Racial Text*. Albany: State University of New York Press.

Gupta, A., and C. Ferguson. 1992. Beyond "Culture": Space, Identity and the Politics of Difference. *Cultural Anthropology* 7 (1): 6–23.

Hall, C. I. 1992. Please Choose One: Ethnic Identity Choices for Biracial Individuals. In M.P.P. Root (ed.), *Racially Mixed People in America*. Newbury Park, Calif.: Sage Publications.

Hall, S. 1994. Cultural Identity and Diaspora. In P. Williams and L. Chrisman (eds.), *Colonial Discourse and Post-Colonial Theory: A Reader*. London: Harvester Wheatsheaf.

Harrison, E. 1994. Principal's Race Comments Spur Small Town Uproar. *Los Angeles Times*, March 16.

Hearst, M. R., ed. (n.d.). *Interracial Identity: Celebration, Conflict, or Choice?: An Anthology*. Chicago: Biracial Family Network.

Hicks, E. 1981. Cultural Marxism: Non-Synchrony and Feminist Practice. In L. Sargeant (ed.), *Women and Revolution*. Boston: South End Press.

Hollinger, D. 1995. *Post-Ethnic America*. New York: Basic Books.

Jacobs, J. H. 1992. Identity Development in Biracial Children. In M.P.P. Root (ed.), *Racially Mixed People in America*. Newbury Park, Calif.: Sage Publications.

Johnson, D. J. 1992. Developmental Pathways: Toward an Ecological Theoretical Formulation of Race Identity in Black–White Children. In M.P.P. Root (ed.), *Racially Mixed People in America*. Newbury Park, Calif.: Sage Publications.

Jones, L. 1995. *Bulletproof Diva : Tales of Race, Sex, and Hair*. New York: Anchor Books.

Kitahara-Kich, G. 1992. The Developmental Process of Asserting a Biracial, Bicultural Identity. In M.P.P. Root (ed.), *Racially Mixed People in America*. Newbury Park, Calif.: Sage Publications.

Kincheloe, J. L., and W. F. Pinar, eds. 1991. *Curriculum as Social Psychoanalysis: The Significance of Place*. Albany: State University of New York Press.

King, R. C., and K. DaCosta. 1996. Changing Face, Changing Race: The Remaking of Race in the Japanese American and African American Communities. In M.P.P. Root (ed.), *The Multiracial Experience: Racial Borders as the New Frontier*. Newbury Park, Calif.: Sage Publications.

Krebs, N. B. 1999. *Edge-Walkers: Defusing Cultural Boundaries on the New Global Frontier.* Far Hills, N.J.: New Horizon Press.

Kriegar, N. 1994. Proposed "Race/Ethnicity" Questionnaire and Data Code Form. Prepared for the OMB hearings regarding OMB's Statistical Policy Directive No. 15, Race and Ethnic Standards for Federal Statistics and Administrative Reporting. 14 July, San Francisco.

LaFromboise, T., H.L.K. Coleman, and J. Gerton. 1993. Psychological Impact of Biculturalism: Evidence and Theory. *Psychology Bulletin* 114 (3): 395–412.

Lave, J., and E. Wenger. 1991. *Situated Learning: Legitimate Peripheral Participation.* Cambridge: Cambridge University Press.

Malkki, L. 1992. National Geographic: The Rooting of Peoples and the Territorialization of National Identity among Scholars and Refugees. *Cultural Anthropology* 7 (1): 24–43.

McCarthy, C. 1988. Rethinking Liberal and Radical Perspectives on Racial Inequality in Schooling: Making the Case for Non-Synchrony. *Harvard Education Review* 58 (3): 265–279.

McCarthy, C., and W. Crichlow, eds. 1993. *Race, Identity and Representation in Education.* New York: Routledge.

McKay, R. B., and M. de la Puente. 1996. Cognitive Testing of Racial and Ethnic Questions in the CPS Supplement. *Monthly Labor Review* 119: 8–12.

Miller, R. L. 1992. The Human Ecology of Multiracial Identity. In M.P.P. Root (ed.), *Racially Mixed People in America.* Newbury Park, Calif.: Sage Publications.

Morrow, R. A., and C. A. Torres. 1995. *Social Theory and Education: A Critique of Theories of Social and Cultural Reproduction.* Albany: State University of New York Press.

Nakashima, C. L. 1992. An Invisible Monster: The Creation and Denial of Mixed-Race People in America. In M.P.P. Root (ed.), *Racially Mixed People in America.* Newbury Park, Calif.: Sage Publications.

Nieto, S. 1992. *Affirming Diversity: The Sociopolitical Context of Multicultural Education.* New York: Longman.

Oetting, E. R. 1993. Orthogonal Cultural Identification: Theoretical Links between Cultural Identification and Substance Use. In M. De La Rosa (ed.), *Drug Abuse among Minority Youth: Advances in Research and Methodology.* Rockville, Md.: National Institute on Drug Abuse.

Office of Management and Budget (OMB). 1997. *Revisions to the Standards for the Classification of Federal Data on Race and Ethnicity.* Washington, D.C. Available online at <http://www.whitehouse.gov/OMB/fedreg/ombdir15.html>.

Ogbu, J. U. 1986. The Consequences of the American Caste System. In U. Neisser (ed.), *The School Achievement of Minority Children: New Perspectives.* Hillsdale, N.J.: Lawrence Erlbaum Associates.

Omi, M. 1997. Racial Identity and the State: The Dilemmas of Classification. *Law and Inequality: A Journal of Theory and Practice* 15 (1): 6–23.

Omi, M., and H. Winant. 1993. On the Theoretical Concept of Race. In C. McCarthy and W. Crichlow (eds.), *Race, Identity and Representation in Education.* New York: Routledge.

———. 1986. *Racial Formation in the United States: From the 1960s to the 1980s*. New York: Routledge and Kegan Paul.

Park, R. E. 1928. Human Migration and the Marginal Man. *American Journal of Sociology* 33 (6): 881–893.

Peshkin, A. 1991. *The Color of Strangers, The Color of Friends: The Play of Ethnicity in School and Community*. Chicago: University of Chicago Press.

Phelan, P., and A. L. Davidson, eds. 1993. *Renegotiating Cultural Diversity in American Schools*. New York: Teachers College Press.

Phinney, J. 1995. At the Interface of Cultures: Multiethnic/Multiracial High School and College Students. *Journal of Social Psychology* 136 (2): 139–158.

———. 1992. The Multigroup Ethnic Identity Measure: A New Scale for Use with Diverse Groups. *Journal of Adolescent Research* 7 (2): 156–176.

Pinar, W. F., and W. M. Reynolds, eds. 1992. *Understanding Curriculum as Phenomenological and Deconstructed Text*. New York: Teachers College Press.

Rich, A. 1986. Invisibility in Academe. In A. Rich (ed.), *Blood, Bread and Poetry: Selected Prose 1979–1985*. New York: W. W. Norton.

Roman, L. 1993. White Is a Color! White Defensiveness, Postmodernism, and Anti-Racist Pedagogy. In C. McCarthy and W. Crichlow (eds.), *Race, Identity and Representation in Education*. New York: Routledge.

Root, M.P.P. 1990. Resolving Other Status: Identity Development of Biracial Individuals. In *Diversity and Complexity in Feminist Theory*. New York: Haworth.

———, ed. 1992. *Racially Mixed People in America*. Newbury Park, Calif.: Sage Publications.

———, ed. 1996. *The Multiracial Experience: Racial Borders as the New Frontier*. Newbury Park, Calif.: Sage Publications.

Ropp, S. M., T. K. Williams, C. T. Rooks, and M. Lee, eds. 1995. *Prism Lives / Emerging Voices of Multiracial Asians: A Selective, Partially Annotated Bibliography*. Los Angeles: UCLA Asian American Studies Center Reading Room/Library.

Roseberry, W. 1992. Multiculturalism and the Challenge of Anthropology. *Social Research* 59 (4): 841–858.

Russell, K., M. Wilson, and R. Hall. 1992. *The Color Complex: The Politics of Skin Color among African Americans*. New York: Anchor Books.

Saluter, A. F. 1992. Marital Status and Living Arrangements: March 1992. *Current Population Reports / Population Statistics*, ser. P-20, no. 468. Washington, D.C.: U.S. Department of Commerce, Bureau of the Census.

Spickard, P. R. 1992. The Illogic of American Racial Categories. In M.P.P. Root (ed.), *Racially Mixed People in America*. Newbury Park, Calif.: Sage Publications.

Spindler, G. D. 1987. *Education and Cultural Process: Anthropological Approaches*. 2d ed. Prospect Heights, Ill.: Waveland Press.

Spindler, G. D., and L. Spindler, eds. 1994. *Pathways to Cultural Awareness*. Thousand Oaks, Calif.: Corwin Press.

———. 1990. *The American Cultural Dialogue and its Transmission*. London: Falmer Press.

Stephan, W. G., and C. W. Stephan. 1991. Intermarriage: Effects on Personality, Adjustment, and Intergroup Relations in Two Samples of Students. *Journal of Marriage and the Family* 53 (1): 241–250.

Stonequist, E. V. 1937. *The Marginal Man: A Study in Personality and Culture Conflict.* New York: Russell and Russell.

Streeter, C. 1996. Ambiguous Bodies: Locating Black/White Women in Cultural Representations. In M.P.P. Root (ed.), *The Multiracial Experience: Racial Borders as the New Frontier.* Newbury Park, Calif.: Sage Publications.

Taubman, P. 1993. Separate Identities, Separate Lives: Diversity in the Curriculum. In L. A. Castanell and W. F. Pinar (eds.), *Understanding Curriculum as Racial Text.* Albany: State University of New York Press; reprint, New York: Routledge.

Thornton, M. 1992. The Quiet Immigration: Foreign Spouses of U.S. Citizens. In M.P.P. Root (ed.), *Racially Mixed People in America.* Newbury Park, Calif.: Sage Publications.

Time. 1993. The New Face of America. Special issue, Fall.

Tucker, C., and B. Kojetin. 1996. Testing Racial and Ethnic Origin Questions in the CPS Supplement. *Monthly Labor Review* 119: 3–7.

Tyack, D. 1993. Constructing Difference: Historical Reflections on Schooling and Social Diversity. *Teachers College Record* 95: 8–34.

Wallace, K. R. 1995. Reflection or Distortion? Student, Teacher and Administrator Perceptions of Mandatory Racial and Ethnic Accounting. Unpublished pilot study, Stanford University.

Waters, M. C. 1990. *Ethnic Options: Choosing Identities in America.* Berkeley and Los Angeles: University of California Press.

West, C. 1993. *Race Matters.* New York: Vintage Books.

Williams, T. K. 1992. Prism Lives: Identity of Binational Amerasians. In M.P.P. Root (ed.), *Racially Mixed People in America.* Newbury Park, Calif.: Sage Publications.

Zack, N. 1995. Mixed Black and White Race and Public Policy. *Hypatia* 10 (1): 120–132.

Index

ABOUT THE AUTHOR

Kendra R. Wallace is Assistant Professor of Education at the University of Maryland, Baltimore County.